CATHOLIC MEN

LIVING THE FAITH

A SMALL
GROUP GUIDE

**STEVE MᶜCOY-THOMPSON
AND RANDY M. HAYKIN**

ave maria press AᴍP notre dame, indiana

© 2008 by Steve McCoy-Thompson and Randy M. Haykin

Founded in 1865, Ave Maria Press is a ministry of the Indiana Province of Holy Cross.

www.avemariapress.com

ISBN-10 1-59471-180-1   ISBN-13 978-1-59471-180-0

Cover design by Brian C. Conley.

Text design by John R. Carson.

Printed and bound in the United States of America.

Contents

● ●

Introduction 1
  Welcome... 1
  Getting Started... 4
  Meetings and Retreats 13
  First Meeting 19
  Check-In Meeting... 23

Centering God and Self.. 27
  1. How Men Find God.. 28
  2. Finding True North... 33
  3. Spiritual Gifts and Talents 40
  4. When Self-Worth Is Challenged 45
  5. Seeking Balance 51
  6. From Success to Significance................................... 55

Nurturing Faith and Family... 61
  1. Faith in the Family 62
  2. Family in Scripture 67
  3. Faith in Our Children.. 72
  4. Faith in Our Partners.. 78
  5. Supporting Our Family's Gifts 84
  6. Faith in Our Fathers.. 89

Balancing Faith and Work 95
  1. Faith in the Workplace 96
  2. Defining Mission... 101
  3. Finding Purpose at Work.. 106

4. Spiritual Leadership 110
5. Taking Stock 114
6. Spiritual Legacy Building 119

Growing Faith in the World 125
1. Individual Service 126
2. Appreciating Other Faiths 132
3. Spiritual Community Leadership 136
4. Wealth and Charity 141
5. Group Community Service 146

Acknowledgments 151

About the Authors 153

Introduction

....

WELCOME

In 2001, our local economy buckled. Friends lost jobs, curtailed family plans, and put their retirement dreams on hold. Many of us were forced to reevaluate personal priorities and even reassess our spiritual values. As men, we responded in typical fashion—we joked on the outside and tried to go it alone.

During this time of turbulence, we took a good look at our own lives. A few years earlier, we had both converted to Catholicism—Steve from a vague agnosticism and Randy from cultural Judaism. The journey to conversion was intense and exhilarating. And, most important of all, we did not go it alone. Our parish community helped every step of the way by hosting a year-long group process that prepared us for the Rite of Christian Initiation of Adults (RCIA). Through this program, we discovered the true power of fellowship—of people joining together to find faith, share doubts, and develop an abiding relationship with God. Naturally, after our initiation into the Church, we wanted to continue this faith journey with others.

During his conversion to Christianity, Randy invited eight men to a simple breakfast meeting to explore the idea of gathering on a regular basis. The goal was not only to share faith, but also to learn from each other in applying the principles of that faith to daily life. Years later, our small band of brothers has grown in numbers and in faith. We call ourselves the Boys of Breakfast, which we'll explain later, and we truly value the relationships we have deepened with one another and with God.

Jesus recognized the power of fellowship. "For where two or three are gathered together in my name, there am I in the midst of them" (Mt 18:20). In other words, we are not meant to go it alone. God provides the gift of relationship so that we might seek the Holy Spirit through and in others. In *Fuel*, we hope to share this gift, with lessons we have learned, topical meeting outlines, and a broad range of resources, so that other men can find what we have found: the grace and the grounding that comes from true camaraderie in Christ.

Why a Men's Group?

Throughout the United States, a growing number of Christians of all denominations are seeing the power of fellowship. They are enhancing their faith *and* their church experience by extending both into the broader community. Men's groups are also growing in number, reflecting our own unique qualities and needs. Though we may sometimes be slow to build relationships, men cherish friendship and a shared sense of purpose. We need spiritual guidance and crave significance and know, down deep, that God holds the answer to both. And we always enjoy sharing a good joke (and maybe a good meal) especially when we're struggling on the inside.

In plain words, a men's faith group speaks to men striving to live their faith. By joining with other men, we enter a broad fraternity of discipleship that goes back two-thousand years to when Jesus sent his disciples forth to announce the Good News. We follow Peter and Paul and millions of other disciples throughout the ages who have tried to live the Word of God in the world. While we may not be headed for sainthood, or even a cushy retirement, we appreciate this call to faith and understand the power of God to transform lives. We know that through brotherhood in Christ, we can become men of God, seeking faith through friendship and learning to be leaders in the Lord. Ultimately, this is why we join. Our own men's group, Boys of Breakfast, helps to provide a roadmap and spiritual fuel for our journeys of faith. We hope that this book and the men's faith group it helps you create and/or sustain do the same for you.

What to Expect

Fuel is the product of six years worth of meetings (and a lot of morning coffee and oatmeal). Our goal is to help men apply the teachings of Christ and the inspired power of God to many of the critical issues we face every day. We have distilled our own lessons learned into four themes that speak to the fundamental concerns and dreams of many men. These themes form the main chapters of this book and build on the call to center ourselves in God, which is fundamental to forging balance and purpose in our daily lives:

1. Centering God and Self
2. Nurturing Faith and Family
3. Balancing Faith and Work
4. Growing Faith in the World

Each theme includes five or six easy-to-follow topical outlines, many of which can be spread over several meetings. When supplemented with the lists of recommended readings at the end of each meeting outline and retreat materials available online, *Fuel* provides guidance and inspiration for as many as one hundred meetings. The meeting format is designed to provide a framework for faith discussion and includes an opening prayer, humor, a relevant quote, Bible passage, a series of reflection questions, and an exercise or exercises to prompt further sharing and exploration. We provide details on this format in the next section.

In the end, we encourage every faith group to chart its own course. Feel free to play around with the work we've prepared and create your own approach as well as new traditions, just as families do with special holidays and events. By working with the meeting outlines, reading suggested reference materials, and using the retreat materials, your group will be well positioned to thrive and to spread the Good News to others. Enjoy this exceptional time together, the sense of shared faith that comes with fellowship, and the realization that you are not, and never have been, expected to go it alone.

GETTING STARTED

Keeping God at the Center

Our own group began slowly, as men are typically slow joiners—unless there's a sport or food involved. Our original purpose was (and still is) to break bread and a few doughnuts together, to share the Word and the Spirit of God, and to realize God's mission for us in the world. For many of us, these morning sessions have helped to anchor our lives by reinforcing the faith we share in God and in each other. After several name changes, including Men of Morning (which yielded an acronym, MoMs, that didn't quite fit), we settled on Boys of Breakfast (with the much manlier BoBs). It wasn't until our second year, however, that we found our true direction, courtesy of a visitor.

We regularly invite guest speakers to our meetings. They provide a fresh voice and keep us on our best behavior. One morning, our associate pastor joined us over scrambled eggs to discuss an issue we'd been grappling with, namely, the constant struggle for balance in life. Many men who are family bread-winners spend fifty to eighty hours per week between work and commute, and the remainder try-

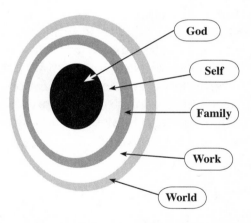

ing to balance family, friends, church, and community. In dual-income families, the challenges are even greater and can be just as daunting for those who are retired, single, widowed, or divorced. No wonder we feel out of balance and sleep-deprived half the time!

Our associate pastor helped us discover a simple truth: The search for balance begins by knowing one's self; and the first step on that journey begins by placing God at the center. All else emanates from this core: a better understanding of our own gifts and talents, and an appreciation of our roles in the family, at work, and in the world. God grounds us, if we allow, and Christ's teachings help guide us to this center.

Of course, this is easier said than done. And, unless you are a dedicated hermit-mystic, it is almost impossible to realize alone. This is where a men's faith group can make a vital contribution. For by seeking God's core with others, we stand a better chance of finding balance in ourselves. Let's get started.

Beginnings

For those who are considering forming a men's fellowship group, the following are lessons we've learned that can help build a meaningful and lasting structure. For those already in a group, these lessons may help strengthen your meetings and promote meaningful communication. While these guidelines have worked well for us, please treat them as suggestions, adapting them to your own situation.

Formation

Men don't tend to initiate faith groups, but they will attend just about anything on a trial basis—particularly if they know one or two of the members. Church leaders, fraternal societies, and small Christian communities can play a vital role as catalysts. A good first step for men who may have trouble with the "C" word (commitment) is to sponsor an open house, a meal (they don't call us Boys of Breakfast for nothing), or an informal meeting. Here, take time to present the idea and the structure of the group and do some good old-fashioned cheerleading to emphasize the importance of understanding faith through the unique concerns and perspectives of men.

The key at this stage is camaraderie; the faith formation and the fellowship will surely follow. Encourage men to invite friends, friends of friends, and others to join in the journey. It is crucial is to make the process safe for men to join and to find another home for their faith.

Leadership

In the early years of group formation, leadership is critical. Each group should have at least one or two people who are willing, committed, and excited to guide the group forward. They will be expected to maintain the group roster, read this guidebook in advance of the sessions, lead the initial sessions, send reminder e-mails between sessions, and continue the cheerleading until the group becomes more participative. Later, as the group stabilizes, others should be encouraged to step forward to lead activities, sessions, and retreats. Find out if your parish offers leadership training for small groups. Other valuable training resources for small Christian communities are available online. Our website, www.faithbalance.com, provides a number of references.

Membership

For any membership group, mutual interest and a strong level of commitment are essential ingredients for success. According to Lloyd Reeb, author of *From Success to Significance*, the most successful groups tend to include members in a similar stage of life such as young parenthood, mid-life, or retirement. At the same time, diversity is important to add both perspective and a fresh voice to group discussions. In our group, the majority of members are Catholic, married with children, and of similar age. At the same time we benefit greatly from older and younger members and by including men from other denominations and faiths, either as guests or permanent members. Their presence both helps to extend the Word of God to others in the community and adds a valuable perspective on God within the group. We provide a sample first meeting beginning on page xxv to help vet some of these issues and to help ensure that people are on the same page at the outset.

Group Size

Many men attend group meetings only as their work, family, and travel schedule allows. This means that 30 to 40 percent of the group may be absent at any given time. Therefore, we recommend forming groups of ten to fifteen people, so that actual attendance is typically a comfortable six to twelve people (we have found that beyond twelve people, the group loses intimacy). In other words, as with party planning, invite more than you expect to attend.

Location

We recommend a comfortable restaurant for a meal meeting, such as breakfast. Most restaurants are happy to set aside table space for regularly scheduled customers, though they may frown if you launch a game of tag football. If a restaurant is not possible, most parishes will provide meeting space as long as you plan ahead, and don't leave crumbs! Or, group members may feel comfortable offering their homes for meetings. Just be sure to rotate the location so that one or two members don't feel like they're serving as den mothers for the rest of the group.

Time

Our group meets at 7 a.m. so as not to interfere with work or family evenings (and to avoid morning exercise). Also consider weekend mornings, or Friday afternoons after work. When selecting a time to meet, listen to the members and choose a time that works for most people most of the time, which is about the best you can do.

Duration

How much time should you allocate? Men are generally busy, or at least they like to *seem* busy, so one hour to ninety minutes per session may be sufficient. What is more important is that you don't cut short discussion concerning any of the topics. If the session runs longer and a few people must leave early, acknowledge that need and pause for them to do so. If you're not able to complete a session in an hour, continue discussion at the next session. Keep people engaged. One of the best ways to do that is to take the time to hear what they have to say.

Setting Ground Rules

These are essential for building trust and should be established at the first official meeting (see page 28). They include the following principles: confidentiality, respectfulness, and general good humor, which is important, especially if you meet in the early morning. Resources are available for meeting management at www.faithbalance.com.

Meeting Format

This book provides a basic meeting format on page 20 to guide the group through a series of sessions. However, we encourage flexibility in adapting to the needs and the interests of your group which, in turn, will evolve over time.

Outside Resources

Fuel includes recommended readings at the end of each topical outline. Our own group often devotes several meetings to a book that a member has enjoyed. Feel free to use these listings for inspiration, though you certainly are not required to do so. We have enough "homework" in our lives! We recommend that the group leader or another member volunteer to review the book first and see if it's appropriate for your group. If the book is chosen, the facilitator may want to create questions or exercises to accompany the book.

Our group has also enjoyed having outside speakers attend our meetings, such as local priests, counselors, authors, or anyone with a unique perspective on faith. We strongly encourage this as a way to inject energy into the group. All group members should be encouraged to identify and propose prospective guest speakers and schedule time for them to visit.

Connecting to Families

Occasionally, it's good to get together with wives, significant others, and the families of group members. Family is an essential part of life for most men, and reinforcing family will actually reinforce the commitment of the men (and the support of their spouses) to the faith group as a whole. The events our group holds with spouses and significant others are among our most memorable and exhilarating activities. Examples of opportunities for get-togethers include a special "happy" hour for group members and their spouses, a gathering around Valentine's Day, or a special dinner for group members and their spouses. When focusing on family life, be sure to incorporate the particular needs and circumstances of all group members whether they are married, single, separated, divorced, or widowed.

Connecting to the World

By reading this book and joining a men's faith group, you are also becoming part of a broader movement that is bringing new energy to Christian faith sharing. Small Christian Communities (SCCs) are emerging throughout the world as a vibrant model of fellowship and service in Christ. Search online for national networking resources in this growing area of Church life or visit www.faithbalance.com.

Managing Expectations

For one of our Boys of Breakfast meetings, we created an exercise called the "Life Metaphor" as a way to place both our personal histories and our goals in perspective. Tom, a founding member of our group, said he saw his life as a baseball game. You often strike out, sometimes you get a hit, and every now and then you swing for the fences. The important thing is to try to get on base, and when you do, to keep moving around the bases, and score.

The same can be said of a men's group. There will be hits and misses and some solid opportunities to score, both spiritually and personally. The important thing is to get people in the game—whether yours is a new group or an existing one. At the same time, it's a good idea to know what to expect once on base. The following are a few tips and pointers to help with both aspects.

First Base

The start-up phase, heading to first, is often character-ized by a combination of interest and wariness. The key at this early stage is to build mutual trust by establishing both ground rules and expectations (we offer a sample first meeting to get this process started). Take time to get to know one another and ensure that everyone is on the same page. If there appear to be fundamental differences about what the group should be and how it should be structured, honor these issues and consider alternatives. This early investment will pay back manyfold.

Second Base

While rounding second base, some men may get distracted or thrown off balance by the competing pressures in their lives. A good way to keep people engaged is to have regular check-ins with the group in order to see if expectations are being met. Practical tips for re-engagement are provided later in this book.

Third Base

By the next phase—heading for third—some groups may experience conflict. This may not occur until the second or third year, but is a normal stage of group development whenever it arises. Some men may voice dissatisfaction or, worse, simply disengage and thus pose a challenge to the group's energy. The best solution is to listen, accommodate when possible, and ultimately let people leave with no hard feelings if that is their choice. Remember that conflict can ultimately make the group stronger and should be addressed in a healthy way. Always leave the door open for anyone who may want to return.

Home Plate

In time, the group should feel like home. Men tend to build bonds through action, so keep the group lively, add some humor, and plan activities outside the group framework when possible. These activities can be service-oriented, helping spread Christ in the world, or simply ways to have fun. In either case, outside activities reinforce the relationships you have made with each other. These, in turn, reinforce your relationship with God.

Finally, it is important to accept that people come and go. Should members move to another city or state, or become too busy at work or at home, they may be forced to leave the group. Keep them on your e-mail list if they want. Offer them best wishes and a prayer and keep the door open for their return. Many will in time. It's also a good idea to seek new members on a regular basis. The trick is getting them to first base while other members may be on third. You may consider a separate meeting for new members with a few men of the old guard to ensure that everyone feels welcome. We also recommend regular check-in sessions (a meeting format is provided on page xx) as a time to both realign your vision for the group and formally introduce new members.

One last thing is necessary and then you'll be as ready as you'll ever be. As with all great adventures, begin in prayer. Offer your group up to God, ask the Holy Spirit for constant guidance, and pass the butter.

MEETINGS AND RETREATS

Fuel provides twenty-three topical outlines that may each last several meetings, along with a broad range of suggested reading materials. In addition, we offer a retreat outline, "Exploring Our Relationships with Our Significant Others," for download at www.avemaria press.com or at www.faithbalance.com. Taken together, *Fuel* delivers as many as a hundred meetings' worth of material—from opening prayers and scriptural references to discussion questions and exercises. Throughout, the materials are designed to be inspirational rather than prescriptive, and we encourage group members to draw from and modify the content to fit their particular needs. Below is our meeting format, along with suggestions for who can do what and when.

Meeting Format
º º º º º º º º º

In our experience, men appreciate structure, particularly as the group is in its formative phase, but also want flexibility to pick and choose content. So, for easy reference and picking, we use a similar, though not identical, pattern for each meeting.

Topic Heading

This is the overall theme for a particular session or series of sessions.

Objective and Preparation

Men typically like to know where they are going and why. Here, we define meeting objectives and indicate any advance preparation that might be needed. The group leader should convey these objectives to the other members by asking them to read this section in advance of the meeting.

Opening Prayer

Ideally, every meeting begins with prayer to ground the group in the Lord's grace. We provide a sample prayer for each topic; however, feel free to create your own. Two of our BoBs members, Mike and Bing, are gifted in prayer and we often ask one of them to lead us in an opening or closing prayer. Look to your own members for inspiration. Often, they are just waiting to be asked.

Humor

Our group enjoys sharing a bit of humor early in each meeting. Laughter can open our minds and hearts to God and make us more receptive to listening. In our group, we even have a designated joke-teller, Ed, who brightens our mornings. We encourage you to find your story- or joke-teller in the group (the Internet offers a wealth of humorous resources). In this book, we offer shorter slices of humor that are tied to the topic and come from some of the wittiest minds in the world. Enjoy!

Guidance

This brief reflection is offered to center the group and get everyone thinking about the topic. We recommend that someone from the group read this reflection aloud. Encourage group discussion of the ideas and the perspectives offered here, some of which are purposely provocative.

Passage from Scripture

This is God's own word on the subject. Read the passage aloud and feel free to discuss at length. Some men may want to read the extended passage from the Bible to appreciate the full story in context. Scriptural references are provided throughout each meeting outline to help men become more familiar with the Bible. We encourage members to seek out these texts, discuss with the group, and explore how they apply to the realities of daily living.

Food for Thought

Greater minds than ours have addressed the themes and the topics presented here. We provide some of their thoughts as inspiration. Again, ask someone to read them aloud and then discuss these further, as you like.

Discussion

What is a faith journey without discussion of our life's big questions? Here, we provide a set of questions to prompt a meaningful exchange of ideas. The meeting leader should read the questions and moderate discussion. Please add your own questions to liven the discussion.

Exercises

We offer a range of group-tested exercises that help members think and engage more deeply concerning each topic.

Journal Notes

Many men like to keep notes or journal, so we provide space within each session outline to do so.

Additional Reading

Here we suggest books and other resources on the topic that group members may find helpful.

Retreats

° ° ° ° ° ° ° ° °

As we mentioned earlier, our group really enjoys and benefits from an annual retreat. We look forward to this chance to get away from the hustle and bustle of life for about thirty hours (all we can afford) and come together in fellowship. Three retreat summaries and a complete retreat outline called "Exploring Relationships with Our Significant Others" are available at www.avemariapress.com. (Additional retreat outlines are also available at www.faithbalance.com). The outline is easy to follow and will help guide the group from start to finish. Note that the retreat can occur at any time but is especially suited to sessions in the chapter on "Nurturing Faith and Family."

To ensure a successful retreat, your group will need to "volunteer" one or two members to serve as retreat leaders. The retreat leaders should review the outline and modify it to suit the needs of the group. To make modification easier, you may download the text, then copy, paste, and edit as much as you like. Prior to the retreat devote at least part of one meeting to going over the proposed outline. Make sure everyone is comfortable with the program, delegate people to lead certain elements of the retreat (one of the perks of being a leader!), and modify again based on member feedback. As for timing, we find it easiest to meet Sunday at noon for lunch and extend to the following Monday afternoon. This helps spread the time away between family and work. But your group may well find other times more suitable.

Don't forget logistics (a downside of being a leader). Make arrangements for a place to hold the retreat such as a group member's house or a local church. If you can't arrange overnight lodging, reserve a good meeting room where you can meet over two days. Also make arrangements for food and, if you choose to go out to dinner, reserve restaurant space. Finally, be sure to read the retreat guidelines for what to bring. You can probably delegate that too!

Check-in Times

While this book does not specify times for group check-ins, they are critical. We recommend that once every three to six months you devote at least part of your meeting to ask if expectations are being met or if members would like to try a new direction for a while, such as a focus on scripture or prayer. If a new direction is called for, set this book aside for a while and pick it up again when everyone is ready. Or, you may want to continue with this book, but jump around from theme to theme depending on member priorities. The more group members feel that their suggestions are being heard, the more they will feel part of the group. A simple outline for a check-in session appears on page xxix.

Member Relevance

The session outlines in the book do not specifically direct attention to individual member concerns. Yet what is faith sharing without human caring? We highly recommend setting aside defined (and limited) meeting time to allow members to share personal issues and to request prayers from the rest of the group. Such prayer requests help unite the group and speak to the power of prayer. Many of our most memorable Boys of Breakfast gatherings involve a group member sharing something (previously unknown) about their life and asking for our prayers, which are readily given.

Changes in Membership
○ ○ ○ ○ ○ ○ ○ ○ ○

Depending on the size and the history of the group, the addition or the departure of a member can change group dynamics. Take a moment to welcome any new members (let them each give a brief overview of family, work, and spiritual journey) and to answer questions they might have concerning ground rules, recent discussions, and any strange quirks current members might have. This is also a good time to nominate prospective member(s) for inclusion, possibly at the next check-in meeting. Finally, for members who have left the group for any reason, offer a prayer for their well-being and their continuing faith journey.

FIRST MEETING

Objective: *To set expectations and structure for the group, establish a few ground rules, and build a foundation of shared faith for all the men present.*

If your group is well established and has already set ground rules and expectations, you may want to skip this meeting and go straight to the topical outlines. However, you may want to refer to the First Meeting discussion questions when new members join.

Preparation

Leaders should come prepared to welcome and encourage the group to enter the journey with trust and enthusiasm.

Opening Prayer

Dear Lord,
We welcome this opportunity to gather
in fellowship
and we ask for your blessing as we begin
this time together.
Watch over us and guide us.
Help us to communicate your Word
and listen to your call.
Keep us bonded in faith and in friendship
as we seek a more meaningful relationship
with you
and better appreciation of your intentions for us.
Amen.

Guidance

We embark on an important journey. It is a journey of faith and of fellowship and, if we stick together, we will find friendship along the way. While our intention is not to transform group members into scripture scholars or preachers, we do believe that camaraderie in the name of Christ will deepen our faith and connect us, through relationship with others, to a more personal relationship with God. In the following meetings, we will address some of the most fundamental issues that confront men of faith today: how to develop a more meaningful rela-tionship with God, how to find spiritual balance among the competing pressures of life, and how to use our unique talents to become spiritual leaders at home, at work, and in the community. We also offer opportunities to use scripture and to explore fundamental questions about how we can live the faith in our daily lives. Above all, we hope to enjoy this time together and with God.

Passage From Scripture

He instructed them to take nothing for the journey but a walking stick—no food, no sack, no money in their belts.

—Mark 6:8

Food for Thought

We are not human beings on a spiritual journey.
We are spiritual beings on a human journey.
—Pierre Teilhard de Chardin

Discussion

In a few words, each member of the group should summarize his personal faith journey. Then, discuss the following items, allowing each member to voice his opinion. If possible, the leader should write the responses on a sheet of paper or a flip chart that everyone can see.

1. What are you looking for now in your faith journey —a deeper relationship with God, a personal relationship with Christ, or to more fully live the Word in your family and community? There are no right answers, of course, as every faith journey is unique. Yet by sharing our vision, we establish a basis for a meaningful present and set a mutual course for a faith-filled future.

2. What do you hope to gain through participation in a men's faith group? Friendship in faith? Closeness with God? Stronger scriptural learning? Greater balance in life? Again, there are no right answers. However, it is important to be clear and honest

at the outset. Remember that faith covers a broad spectrum, and so does this book! If your expectations are not met immediately, have patience, talk to the group leader and other members, and try to incorporate your own desires into future agendas. If your hopes and desires are still not met, perhaps God has other plans for you—including forming your own faith group. In all cases, keep communication open and let the Holy Spirit be your guide.

Exercises

A group leader should facilitate discussion on the following items and write responses on a sheet of paper or flip chart so all can see. If possible, come to agreement on these items during the meeting. If not, the leader can propose a resolution based on group responses and e-mail it to everyone in the group for general review and agreement.

1. Setting Ground Rules

   Just as good fences can make for good neighbors, sensible ground rules provide a platform for meaningful discussion and relationship. We recommend establishing the following:

   - Respect other people's opinions.
   - Commit to regular attendance.
   - Keep the group leader informed of any absences.
   - Ensure that all confidences shared during the meeting are kept truly confidential.
   - Propose your own ground rules based on group needs and requirements.

2. Role Definition

We recommend having one or two group leaders for every group. Leaders will typically facilitate communication between and during group meetings, arrange the meeting location, and ensure that any necessary meeting materials are provided. The leader or a delegate should lead the Discussion and the Exercise. Leaders may also suggest that the group spend several meetings with a particular book, as listed in the reference section, to delve more deeply into a particular subject. Other group members should be encouraged to lead Opening Prayer, tell a personal joke (the Humor sections in the book are for inspirational purposes), read aloud, and join in discussing the Guidance section.

Feel free to skip or expand on any of these roles as the Spirit moves and the men discern. Roles can and should evolve as the group evolves and gains or loses members. A good time to address role definition is during Check-in Meetings, which we outline next.

CHECK-IN MEETING

Objective and Preparation

We recommend periodic check-ins about once every three to six months to reconfirm objectives, to see how group members are doing, and to make course corrections as necessary. Check-in sessions also provide a chance for group members to reconnect on a personal level—to share family and work concerns, and to ask for prayers. Finally, check-in time can provide a nice opportunity to

formally introduce new members or to consider prospective members. As these sessions can last anywhere from
fifteen to fifty minutes and may be inserted into a regular
session, we will dispense with the usual meeting format
and simply offer questions to prompt discussion and
sharing and then offer brief ideas about how to handle
membership changes.

Opening Prayer

Dear Lord,
We praise you for granting us this time together.
Thank you for blessing us with the fellowship of
this group of men.
Help us today to let you know what is on our
minds and in our hearts
and to discern how our faith journey is progressing
at home, at work, and in our community.
Help us focus our thoughts on those most in
need.
In your name we pray.
Amen.

Discussion (*A group leader should lead this conversation
and encourage input from all present.*)

1. Are your personal and faith objectives being met, or
   at least addressed, in the context of this men's faith
   group? If so, explain how. If not, try to be specific
   regarding your concerns.

2. Are there aspects of the group meetings you would
   like to improve or expand such as prayer time,
   open discussion, or scripture reading? Would you
   like to change the meeting format?

3. Are there spiritual, doctrinal, or biblical subjects you would like to explore at a deeper level such as Church teaching on a particular issue or a faith tradition you would like to explore? This is also a good time to recommend readings you believe the group would enjoy.

4. How are things going at home? How's work? Those who are comfortable doing so should share their concerns with the group. (Remind the group that everything said in the meetings is strictly confidential. And remember the true power of prayer to change lives. Offer one up to any and all who need one.)

Centering God and Self

Topics

1. How Men Find God
2. Finding True North
3. Spiritual Gifts and Talents
4. When Self-Worth Is Challenged
5. Seeking Balance
6. From Success to Significance

1.

HOW MEN FIND GOD

For one meeting

Objective: *To share experiences and find common ground in our search for God.*

Preparation

Come to the meeting prepared to share the story of how and why you considered joining a men's faith group. How is this part of your broader faith journey? What do you hope to find in the group and on your journey?

Opening Prayer

My Lord God, I have no idea where I am going.
I do not see the road ahead of me.
I cannot know for certain where it will end.
Nor do I really know myself,
and the fact that I think that I am following your will
does not mean that I am actually doing so.
But I believe that the desire to please you does in fact please you.
And I hope I have that desire in all that I am doing.

—Thomas Merton

Humor

> I admire the serene assurance of those who have religious faith. It is wonderful to observe the calm confidence of a Christian with four aces.
>
> —Mark Twain

Guidance

How do men find God? We find God alone and in groups. We find God at work and on the sports field, especially when we pray for miracles. And we find God at home, out in nature and, occasionally, in traffic. There is no universal avenue or end point where all men find God, but there is one constant. We find God in the way that we seek God. God is everywhere and is waiting for us to find him in the most public and private of places. The key, of course, is to *engage* in the search, which is why we gather together. This men's faith group, if we invest in it, can be one way to bring God into our lives and our lives into God.

As we share our experiences, we will see that we are not alone in our search *and our struggle* for a closer relationship with God. We may be stunningly different on the outside, and even odd—like that one guy with a penchant for scrambled eggs and ketchup—but we share many of the same concerns and longings, such as for a solid family and a meaningful life. We also long for a solid relationship with God. This is the glue that holds these groups together. This commonality is where we begin faith formation with our fellow men. The important thing is to communicate, for that is how we come to know each other and, through others, come to more fully know God.

Passage From Scripture

I say to you, if two of you agree on earth about anything for which they are to pray, it shall be granted to them by my heavenly Father. For where two or three are gathered together in my name, there am I in the midst of them.

—Matthew 18:19–20

Food for Thought

When you want to work for God . . . start a committee. When you want to work with God . . . start a prayer group.

—Corrie ten Boom

Discussion and Journaling *(as group or in pairs)*

1. How do you find God? How has this changed over time, from childhood to now? Do you look to God for guidance more or less often than when you were young? Have you left something behind in your relationship with God over the years? What have you gained? What do you want to change, to grow? Where would you like to be in your faith?

2. Share a favorite scripture passage or a prayer, a saint or a sacrament that you may reflect on during the course of the day—the Serenity Prayer when counseling a friend, the beatitudes when setting priorities, or the sacrament of reconciliation after a tough meeting. We have much to learn from each other in this regard, especially the ways other men seek God and, thus, find themselves in the process.

Exercises *(leader led)* ·

Sometimes we seek God and receive the guidance we need (Salvation). Other times we seem to receive no response (Silence). And sometimes, God finds us when we are not looking, in the most unexpected ways (Surprise). On a flip chart, white board, or even a large napkin, write these typical responses to prayer as column headings: Salvation, Silence, and Surprise. Take a few moments to discuss your experience with all three of these responses to prayer, using the suggested questions below.

How do you typically seek God? Through prayer, activity, fellowship? Do you honestly feel God's presence during these times? If so, consider ways that you might reinforce these moments in order to reinforce God's active presence in your life. If not, discuss what might be missing.

Identify a time when you made a clear prayer request for a specific outcome. Describe what happened—was God's response clear or unclear, or did God seem absent? Beneath the column headings identified above, write the prayer request(s) beneath the response(s) that you experienced. Has your experience affected the way you approach God now?

Is there a pattern in the way you seek God? With specific prayer requests or general prayer for guidance? Are you able to discern God's response? Consider ways that we might be more attentive to God's true calling for us.

Is there a pattern in the way God seems to find you? In quiet moments or with family?

Are there patterns in your relationship with God that you would like to change?

Journal Notes

Additional Reading

The Hidden Value of a Man by Gary Smalley and John
    Trent
"How Men Find God," in St. Anthony Messenger, August
    2000
The Christian Husband by Bob Lepine
The Seasons of a Man's Life by Daniel J. Levinson

2.

FINDING TRUE NORTH

For two or more meetings

Objective: *To identify a personal true north as a way of expressing and navigating one's own faith journey.*

Preparation

Prepare for the meetings by making copies for each member of the following "star" image (also available at www.avemariapress.com). Or, each member can sketch his own star on a piece of paper and bring it to the meetings. Group members will be writing notes on each side of the star, so leave some room in the margins.

For the first session, we will attempt to define our own true north as a means to share where we've been and where we want to go in our relationship with God. For the second session, we will identify what strengthens or diminishes our faith, and discuss ways we can keep centered on the journey forward. The goals are to share what we have found on our journey, what we hope to find, and to name what help we can use along the way.

Opening Prayer

Lord God,
we are unsure of the path that you want us to take
and even in which direction to turn.
Yet we know that you will deliver us on the path that is truly right
in your plan for us.
Help us stop and ask you for directions
and then listen to them when you whisper to us.
Help us be obedient to your call.
In your name we pray.
Amen.

Humor

> Thanks to the Interstate Highway System, it is now possible to travel from coast to coast without seeing anything.
>
> —Charles Kuralt

Guidance

Stars have guided travelers for millennia. Using "celestial navigation," a good sextant, and an accurate clock, people have used the stars to navigate across oceans and deserts beneath the dark of night. Yet to make night navigation possible, travelers need a constant—a bearing point by which to steer through the darkness to their destination. The magi of Matthew's Gospel followed a distant star to find the infant Son of God. And, before the Civil War, Harriet Tubman guided slaves to freedom by following the North Star.

We will use the star as a symbol for the long journey to continuous conversion. It is a constant to keep us on the right path. Like Tubman, we have the opportunity to follow a great light of faith that propels us across our own self-doubts to lasting freedom. Like the magi, we must approach that faith in single steps, in order to pursue a promise that seems to shine from within, compelling us forward.

As we navigate personal issues as well as family and work obligations, we travel as seekers in every sense of the word. Along the way, we will face obstacles to living a deeper faith—from a simple lack of time for prayer to anger concerning a recent loss. If we are lucky, we will find sources of inspiration to keep us going. It is therefore essential that we recognize what strengthens and diminishes our faith, and keep our eyes firmly fixed on the light of Christ every step of the way. For like all nighttime travelers, we need a stable, constant light to guide us through the darkness.

Passage From Scripture

After their audience with the king they set out.
And behold, the star that they had seen at its
rising preceded them, until it came and stopped
over the place where the child was. They were
overjoyed at seeing the star, and on entering the
house they saw the child with Mary his mother.
They prostrated themselves and did him hom-
age. Then they opened their treasures and offered
him gifts of gold, frankincense, and myrrh.

—Matthew 2:9–11

Food for Thought

If I had my life to live over I'd like to make more
mistakes next time. I'd relax. I would limber up.
I would be sillier than I have been this trip. I
would take fewer things seriously. I would take
more chances. I would climb more mountains
and swim more rivers. I would eat more ice
cream and fewer beans, I would perhaps have
more actual trouble, but I'd have fewer imagi-
nary ones. . . . If I had to do it again, I would
travel lighter than I have. If I had my life to live
over, I would start barefoot earlier in the spring
and stay that way later in the fall.

—Nadine Stair

Exercises *(leader led, followed by discussion with suggested
questions below)*

Alpha and omega are the first and last letters of the
Greek alphabet. From the earliest years of Christianity,
the Church has used these letters to signify Christ as eternal truth, the beginning and the end of all things. "'I am
the Alpha and the Omega,' says the Lord God, 'the one

who is and who was and who is to come, the almighty'"
(Rv 1:8).

In the following exercises, we apply this symbolism to
our personal journey in faith. The star provides a visual
tool to help us see where we've come from and where we
might be heading. Take a few minutes, alone or in pairs,
to complete the following.

*(We recommend completing steps 1 and 2 below during the
first meeting for this topic and then doing steps 3 and 4 for the
second meeting. Take the time to discuss and share your findings. They will provide a focus for ongoing prayer as the other
group members help to support your journey.)*

1. Label the southern point of the star as the alpha
   point of your spiritual journey. Below the alpha
   point, list your early impressions of God. In other
   words, how did you begin? Was God vague, clear,
   close, distant, comforting, or forbidding like a stern
   old man ready to pass judgment?

2. Now, label the northern point as the omega, the
   goal. Here, identify the relationship you would
   like to have. What are the main qualities of that
   relationship—trust, love, constancy, comfort, hope?
   Discuss the differences between these points and
   how you hope to get from "here" to "there."

3. On the left or western point of the star, list the people, places, and things that reinforce a closer relationship with God. These might be time for prayer,
   going to church, a family outing, or a favorite fish-
   ing hole. Discuss how you can integrate these elements more fully into your life.

4. On the right or eastern side, list what detracts
   from this relationship—your commute, unresolved

family issues, general apathy, anger or resentment toward co-workers or family members. Discuss how you can address these issues, and how you can utilize the positive elements from step three to enable the journey to your omega point with God.

The result of this exercise should be, at a minimum, a clearer understanding of what helps and what hinders your journey to become more centered in God. The key, of course, is to reinforce the former and address the latter. The discussion questions below will help to begin that process.

Discussion and Journaling *(as group or in pairs)*

1. For the first session, take time to discuss any or all of the following questions. Describe your alpha point in developing a personal relationship with God. In other words, what first compelled you on this journey of faith? Was it your parents, a spouse, an important event? What was the relationship like at first? Next discuss how that relationship is now. How has it evolved over time? Is God closer or further from your heart and soul than when you began? Now describe your omega point with God. How you would like that relationship to be—constant, energizing, positive, a source for cen-teredness in the chaos of life? Try to focus on this personal True North—it will help get us where we want to go.

2. For the second session, discuss the western and eastern points on your star. You may find that you share many of the same issues with others in the group. Share how you can accentuate the positive and eliminate, or at least address, the negative. Recognize that both points are critical. We must be

aware of the steps and the stones along our path to true north, lest we get lost or sidetracked along the way. As you reflect on these elements, do you believe there is need for a course correction?

3. If you have time, discuss the meaning of Christ's instructions to his disciples, as indicated in the passage from scripture on page 9. What does Christ mean? If we were planning our own journey in faith, what would we take?

Journal Notes

Additional Reading

First Things First by Stephen R. Covey, A. Roger Merrill, and Rebecca R. Merrill

True North: Discover Your Authentic Leadership by Bill George

Focusing by Eugene T. Gendlin

3.

SPIRITUAL GIFTS
AND TALENTS

For two or more meetings

Objective: *To help us see our own gifts more clearly and to have a better understanding of what we can realistically do with them.*

Preparation

To prepare for these meetings, ask group members to familiarize themselves with the spiritual gifts of God as they are commonly defined. Read Romans 12, 1 Corinthians 12, and Ephesians 4 for reference. The key is to recognize that we each have a unique combination of gifts and that we give thanks to God by cherishing and using them.

Opening Prayer

Lord, make me an instrument of your peace;
where there is hatred, let me sow love;
where there is injury, pardon;
where there is doubt, faith;
where there is despair, hope;
where there is darkness, light;
and where there is sadness, joy.
O Divine Master,
grant that I may not so much seek to be consoled
as to console;
to be understood, as to understand;

to be loved, as to love;
for it is in giving that we receive;
it is in pardoning that we are pardoned,
and it is in dying that we are born to eternal
life.
Amen.

—The Peace Prayer of St. Francis

Humor

I am no more humble than my talents require.

—Oscar Levant

Guidance

In our own men's group, the Boys of Breakfast, two questions keep popping up. First, "How do we recognize our God-given gifts and talents?" The second and perhaps more challenging question is: "What do we do with them?" In other words, among all the competing noises of our lives, how can we discern God's call for us?

The Church has long recognized Seven Gifts of the Holy Spirit, which are rooted in Isaiah 11:2–3. These are: wisdom, understanding, knowledge, counsel (also called right judgment), fortitude, piety (or reverence), and fear of the Lord, which is also called wonder and awe in God. In the thirteenth century, St. Thomas Aquinas taught that these gifts are given by God to provide the inner 'Christ-likeness' that helps us to develop a closer relationship to God. In addition, Paul outlines another set of gifts, sometimes called charisms, that are to be shared with the world. These charisms are cited in Romans 12, 1 Corinthians 12 (cited in the Passage from Scripture below), and Ephesians 4. There are other, more contemporary, spiritual gift inventories that identify charisms ranging from administration and leadership to craftsmanship and healing. In other words, there are enough gifts to go around and to help us find our place in God's light. The important thing is to recognize that we have been given certain gifts and, through prayer and good counsel, we are called to make those gifts manifest both in our hearts and out in the world.

Passage From Scripture

There are different kinds of spiritual gifts but the same Spirit;
there are different forms of service but the same Lord;
there are different workings but the same God who produces all of them in everyone.
To each individual the manifestation of the Spirit is given for some benefit.
To one is given through the Spirit the expression of wisdom; to another the expression of knowledge according to the same Spirit;
to another faith by the same Spirit; to another gifts of healing by the one Spirit;
to another mighty deeds; to another prophecy; to another discernment of spirits; to another varieties of tongues; to another interpretation of tongues.
But one and the same Spirit produces all of these, distributing them individually to each person as he wishes.

—1 Corinthians 12:4–11

Food for Thought

What you are is God's gift to you; what you make of it is your gift to God.

—Fr. Anthony Dalla Villa
Eulogy for Andy Warhol, April 1987

Discussion and Journaling *(may be spread over two meetings)*

Review the range of gifts outlined in the Guidance section above and discuss, as a group or in pairs, the following questions.

1. Can charisms be developed over time? Can one learn to be a healer or a communicator? Can someone learn to be a leader? What charisms, if any, would you like to develop?

2. Discuss the obstacles that may "keep your light under a bushel." Reflect on the obstacles identified in the True North exercise. There may be some important similarities. Discuss how you might address these obstacles—at home, work, or anywhere—in order to realize God's gifts.

3. Ask the group members to identify a gift that seems absent or lacking in their lives at the moment. Perhaps it is an understanding of God's intentions or a lack of wonder and awe in God. Discuss how you might rekindle the flame.

Exercises *(leader led, one for each meeting)*

1. Sometimes it is hard for us to identify our own gifts or charisms, much less act on them. This exercise provides outside help for the task. Provide each member with a sheet of paper and ask him to write his name at the top. Below the name, have each member write a gift, a talent, or a charism that he believes he has. Now have each person pass his sheet to the right. The next person should write a talent or a gift he sees in the named person. Continue around the room and be as complimentary

as you can manage. When the labeling is complete, return the sheets to their owners. Read them aloud or, if too embarrassing, take home and pray over them. The goal is to see ourselves as others do, for there is often more to us than we ourselves realize.

2. During the break between the recommended two meetings, think about the insights you have received from others. Consider and pray over ways that you can build on these insights and utilize the gifts and talents that your group has identified in you. How can you use these at home, at work, and in the community? For the second meeting, share your thoughts with the group as a whole, or in pairs. In subsequent themes and meetings, the group will explore ways to connect God's gifts to God's purpose. For now, it is enough to realize that we do have much to offer in the world.

Journal Notes

Additional Reading

The Purpose-Driven Life: What on Earth Am I Here For? by Rick Warren, pp. 227–256

Thanks! by Robert Emmons

WHEN SELF-WORTH IS CHALLENGED

For one or two meetings

Objective: *To define self-worth, to share struggles that we (or a loved one) may be having in this area, and to seek guidance from scripture.*

Don't worry—this is not meant to be a confession of weakness, which most men would not admit to under torture. Rather, it is an open recognition of our own, or a loved one's, potential and how that may not be being fulfilled in the present.

Preparation

Prior to this session, each group member should select a story from the Bible that either resonates with his own experience at some time in his life or provides inspiration when his own Promised Land seems far away. We mention a few examples in the Guidance section below, but encourage you to seek your own.

Opening Prayer

The day awaits as I open my eyes from sleep,
help me to see you in everyone and everything I encounter today.
I stand before you this day unaware of your will for me.
Lead me to opportunities where I can embrace the challenge to serve you.

Give me the strength to accept those opportunities
with a loving heart
and an outstretched hand.
Be with me, through the obstacles, frustrations,
and rewards that this day will hold.
And give me the wisdom to find peace, even
amidst chaos.
May the morning air bring life to my body and
joy to my soul.
Amen.

—Jenny Tighman
University of Notre Dame

Humor

To love oneself is the beginning of a lifelong
romance.

—Oscar Wilde

Guidance

We all feel lost from time to time because of family
troubles, dissatisfaction at work, or wrestling with our
personal demons. Yet we are taught from an early age
that God is always with us to guide us, if we only seek
him. Ironically, this combination can leave us feeling
both lost *and* guilty. Lost because we are only human
and life weighs on us, and guilty because somehow deep
inside we still believe that good Christians never doubt
God's true purpose, or feel uncertain about the true path
to grace. As men, who tend to internalize and mask our
troubles, this combination can be crippling. Heck, we
have a hard enough time asking directions, much less
seeking help for ourselves, or for friends and family. The
result can be a sense of disconnectedness from the love
of God, which is precisely what we need to keep going
in life.

Fortunately, scripture is filled with people like us who feel lost, have doubts, and sometimes even wail and gnash their teeth. When we read the Bible, we tend to see only the master plan—as if people's journeys are part of a long, smooth road toward grace. But if you were to ask Abraham, Moses, Jesus, Paul, or any of the prophets and apostles, they would tell an entirely different story. Abraham was an average farmer for decades before God spoke to him. Moses did see God, but never the Promised Land for which he longed. Jesus felt forsaken in his final hours of torment. Paul despaired many times that the early Christian communities just weren't getting it. There are many other examples and we invite you to find inspiration in the words of God, for they can teach us a great deal when our own self-worth is challenged.

Passage From Scripture

Are not two sparrows sold for a small coin? Yet not one of them falls to the ground without your Father's knowledge. Even all the hairs of your head are counted. So do not be afraid; you are worth more than many sparrows.

—Matthew 10:29–31

Food for Thought

I don't know if I continue, even today, always liking myself. But what I learned to do many years ago was to forgive myself. It is very important for every human being to forgive herself or himself because if you live, you will make mistakes—it is inevitable. . . . If we all hold on to the mistake, we can't see our own glory in the mirror because we have the mistake between our faces and the mirror; we can't see what we're capable of being.

You can ask forgiveness of others, but in the end
the real forgiveness is in one's own self.

—Maya Angelou

Discussion *(as group or in pairs)*

1. People may have very different definitions of self-worth and the role it plays in their lives. Some are consumed by such issues while others hardly think about them. How do you define self-worth? Is self-worth the same as self-esteem, or self-confidence? How much of your self-worth is defined by other people's impressions; how much comes from within? What role does, and should, God's love play?

2. What would God say? Imagine a conversation with God, which is really another term for prayer. Imagine God's response to this simple question: "What am I worth?" Or, to put it another way, "What is my value on earth?" How might God respond to you? Perhaps more importantly, would you trust that response?

3. Allow each member of the group to discuss a section of the Bible that speaks to them of comfort and hope in times of trouble. There are many examples, since scripture is full of people in trouble! Think of Daniel in the lion's den; Job being stripped of all he holds dear; Jonah running from his problems only to find himself inside a whale; Joseph and his beautiful coat being cast out by his brothers; or any number of prophets who are ignored by their people. The Bible is, in many respects, a story of people just like us. Is there a story of struggle that has resonated with you at some time in your life?

4. For those men who are willing, tell about a time when your sense of purpose or self-worth or faith has been challenged. Perhaps there have been times at home or at work. You likely will find that you're not alone. To the extent that sharing does occur, listen respectfully, maintain confidentiality, and offer prayer and anything else that comes to mind. This is a group in which to foster belief, not just in God but also in each other.

Exercise *(leader led, followed by discussion with suggested questions below)*

Belief in God and in one's self takes effort. Believing is something in which we must actively engage. Sometimes it involves taking on something new, making time for something almost forgotten, or letting go of something that diminishes our faith and ourselves. For this exercise, try to remember the issues discussed in the True North session, particularly the things that enhance or diminish your faith.

In this exercise, we draw a connection between faith and self-worth. As the light of God shines most brightly when it shines within us, so does self-worth. Both can be either enhanced or diminished by certain events (prayer time vs. constant deadlines), people (friendship vs. an abusive boss), or places (nature vs. the slow lane in a long commute). In your journal, on a piece of paper, or in conversation with a partner, identify those things and relationships that help and harm your sense of self-respect. They may concern family, work, church, or the simple act of building muscle around the waistline. Consider how you can make a conscious effort to reinforce those elements that build self-worth. For if God truly shines through us, then we do service to God by helping our selves.

Journal Notes

Additional Reading

Improving Your Self Image by H. Norman Wright
Making Peace with Yourself by Harold Bloomfield

5.

SEEKING BALANCE

For one meeting

Objective: *To begin exploring how we, as men, can center ourselves in God as a necessary step in finding the balance we seek in life.*

Preparation

Men should come to this session prepared to discuss the ways in which their lives may be out of balance. The session will include discussion of ways we can seek to center ourselves during the course of a day and will close with the formation of simple prayer partnerships to help ground us in the coming weeks.

Opening Prayer

Lord, we often find ourselves out of balance in this world
with its constant demands of family, work, and community.
We know that you are the True North on whom we rely
to find our way back to balance.
Help us seek you out in times when we need more balance,
and to understand issues related to better balancing our lives.
Help us be true leaders in all aspects of our lives
by living more balanced lives.
Amen.

Humor

An angel of the Lord came to a man in a dream and gave him three great burdens, in the shape of balls. The man was instructed to walk with these burdens across a high wire that was stretched over a canyon. To make things more difficult, the angel told the man that he was allowed to hold only one burden at a time—much as in real life. The man looked down at the canyon and claimed the task was impossible. Either he or the other two balls would fall into the abyss. The angel smiled and said, "Learn to juggle."

Guidance

As the great painter Henri Matisse once said, "What I dream of is an art of balance." For many men, the illusive dream is a life of balance. If there is one thing most men can agree on, it is that they struggle to find such balance. Between work, family, health, and other obligations, we are constantly juggling. The reality is that most of us only find balance in rare moments: like a family vacation, dinner with a loved one, or sharing an especially good joke with friends. Balance, it seems, comes and goes quite fleetingly. How can we find centeredness amid the chaos of life?

One step toward this elusive sense of balance, and toward deeper relationship with Christ, is to realize we cannot possibly go it alone. Our problems, no matter how fast we juggle, are simply too much to handle by ourselves. While God cannot magically solve our problems, we are foolish to attempt solutions to them without God. Christ waits for us to seek him, through prayer and through relationships with others. As we find in Proverbs 16:11, "Balance and scales belong to the Lord; all the weights used with them are his concern." In other words,

God is central to the question of balance, for the Lord is the scale. We will do well to take our measure in Him.

Passage From Scripture

> May the LORD, our God, be with us as he was with our fathers and may he not forsake us nor cast us off.
> May he draw our hearts to himself, that we may follow him in everything and keep the commands, statutes, and ordinances which he enjoined on our fathers.
>
> —1 Kings 8:57–58

Food For Thought

> Chaos is the score upon which reality is written.
>
> —Henry Miller

Discussion *(as group or in pairs)*

1. In what ways does your life seem in balance? In what ways does it seem out of balance? We all have a litany of causes to choose from—time, money, relationships, work, and prestige—pick one, or all of the above! The important point is to share these pressures with the group so that God and other men may enter more fully into the equation. As you discuss, honestly assess the degree to which you feel that God has been present, or absent, in seeking balance.

2. If you were able (or forced) to give up one thing pulling your life out of balance, what would that be? A mortgage? Business travel? Too much television? Family resentments? What would be the consequences? If God were a life coach, what might he recommend?

Exercises *(leader led)*

Divide the group into pairs. Take a few minutes to share with your partner those issues in faith, family, work, etc. that may be throwing you off balance. You should each write the other's issues on a card and then make a simple promise: to pray for your partner and to keep in touch, via e-mail, phone, or whatever method is most appropriate. The result, in simple terms, is a partnership that should last for as long as the group chooses. To the extent that you are comfortable, you may share these issues and prayers with the other members of the group. Remember that all such confidences within the group are just that: strictly confidential.

Journal Notes

Additional Reading

Balancing Your Family, Faith & Work by Pat Gelsinger

6.

FROM SUCCESS
TO SIGNIFICANCE

For two to three meetings

Objective: *To help group members distinguish between traditional definitions of success, which can be artificial and leave one feeling empty, and a life of true significance.*

Preparation

Prepare for the first meeting by reflecting on how you want to be remembered.

Opening Prayer

Lord, we are blessed to have received so much from you—
our health, our family and friends, our gifts and talents, and our work.
We ask you to help us recognize the successes in our lives
and to open our hearts to new opportunities to realize significance
at home, at work, and in our communities.
Amen.

Humor

I am ready to meet my Maker. Whether my Maker is prepared for the great ordeal of meeting me is another matter.

—Winston Churchill

Passage From Scripture

Thus says the LORD: Let not the wise man glory
in his wisdom, nor the strong man glory in his
strength, nor the rich man glory in his riches;
But rather, let him who glories, glory in this, that
in his prudence he knows me,
Knows that I, the LORD, bring about kindness,
justice and uprightness on the earth;
For with such am I pleased, says the LORD.
—Jeremiah 9:22–23

Guidance

Men are programmed from an early age to distinguish
between success and failure—at sports, at school, and
eventually at work and in adult life. Unfortunately, this
is a Madison Avenue distinction that distracts us from
God's true purpose for us. Christian discipleship on the
other hand calls us to love and serve God and to love
our neighbors *as ourselves*, which is why the concept of
self-worth is so important (see topic 4: When Self-Worth
Is Challenged). The extent to which we do this will form
the foundation for our lasting legacy, our real measure of
success. In these meetings, we provide an opportunity
for group members to explore God's desire for us to
move beyond a narrow definition of success and toward
a better appreciation of true significance.

Talking about significance and practicing it are very
different things. To focus on significance is to focus outside one's self—to see the impact we have on others,
positive or negative. Even the smallest act, a kindness
to a co-worker or patience with a family member, can
have ripple effects far beyond our own horizon. Chaos
Theory presents an excellent model for unimagined
and unintended consequences. It's called the Butterfly
Effect. According to this model, the flutter of a butterfly

can create tiny changes in the atmosphere that may ultimately cause a tornado to appear (or prevent a tornado
from appearing). Here, the flapping wings represent a
small change that causes a chain of events leading to a
major event. The Bible has been describing Chaos Theory
for millennia. A fight between brothers Cain and Abel,
for example, profoundly changed the course of human
history.

When we think of our impact on the world, our
own legacy for unseen generations to come, we need to
appreciate this "law" of unimagined consequences. Our
actions do have untold impacts, whether we realize them
or not. They may not be measurable on the balance sheet
of business or of life, but they matter to the extent that
they perpetuate God's grace in the world. These meetings invite you to take the time to imagine your
consequences in the world and to shape your actions
more carefully, beginning now.

Food for Thought

> The significance of a man is not in what he
> attains, but rather what he longs to attain.
>
> —Kahlil Gibran

Exercises and Discussion *(over several meetings, in pairs or
small groups, then in the large group)*

First Meeting Exercise

1. Think about the last funeral or memorial service
   you attended. Now, without getting too morose,
   take a few minutes to write notes for your own
   eulogy. What would people say about you if you
   died today?

2. Is this a list of successes or significances or both? What is left when you strip away conventional measures of success?

First Meeting Discussion Questions
(for the whole group)

To the extent that you are comfortable, share some of your notes. Then ask and try to answer the following questions.

1. How might your life be different if you focused on "significance" as opposed to "success"?

2. What role has social justice or service played in your accomplishments?

3. Are you able to recognize opportunities for significance? What role do you think God plays in bringing these opportunities into your life? Does prayer help in this regard? How do you respond?

Second Meeting Exercise

During the intervening period between meetings, reflect on your eulogy notes from the first exercise. Try to actually write it. Be as sappy and heartfelt as you'd like—after all, it's your funeral! But be sincere as well, after all you've invited a lot guests (keep in mind that famous people do this all the time!). Be sure to include what you would like someone to say regarding your true significance.

Second Meeting Discussion Questions

1. Did your eulogy change upon further reflection? To the extent that you want, share those changes with the group.

2. What do you understand "leaving a legacy" to your family, your work colleagues, or your community to mean?

3. Identify three meaningful relationships or opportunities in life where you can make a positive difference, starting today.

4. Has God prepared you for opportunities for significance by giving you unique talents? What are these and how do you try to use them wisely?

Journal Notes

Additional Reading

Half Time by Bob Buford
From Success to Significance by Lloyd Reeb
Secrets of the Vine: Breaking Through to Abundance by Bruce
    Wilkinson
The Five People You Meet in Heaven by Mitch Albom

Nurturing Faith and Family

Topics

1. Faith in the Family
2. Family in Scripture
3. Faith in Our Children
4. Faith in Our Partners
5. Supporting Our Family's Gifts
6. Faith in Our Fathers

1.

FAITH IN THE FAMILY

For two meetings

Objective: *To begin exploring the distinctions between the ideals and realities of daily family life.*

This meeting introduces the theme of Nurturing Faith in the Family, provides an opportunity for group members to meet each other's families, to discuss the role of men in family faith formation, and to offer prayers for guidance because we know we're going to need it!

Preparation

Come to the first meeting prepared to discuss your image of the perfect family and how that has evolved over time. If you have single men in your group, or men who are not fathers, you will need to adapt some of the materials presented below to better incorporate the realities of their daily lives and their experience of family.

Opening Prayer

Dear Lord, you have given the gift of family.
Sometimes, we fail to recognize that gift or
appreciate its true value.
We ask for your help, Lord, in learning to
appreciate the love and commitment
that are the foundation for family life.
We ask for your guidance in helping us guide
our own families,
however they may be defined,

in building closer relationships with each other
and with you, dear God.
Amen.

Humor

Having a family is like having a bowling alley
installed in your brain.

—Martin Mull

Guidance

Often we feel that we will never reach the ideal family, that postcard image in which father actually does
know best and the kids listen to him! Yet no matter how
imperfect, it is important to remember that our families
are holy, for they are gifts of God. They are also fundamental to our personal well-being and to our future. As
Pope John Paul II stated, "As the family goes, so goes the
nation and so goes the whole world in which we live." In
other words, as maddening as families can sometimes be,
they deserve our greatest attention. While we may never
reach the ideal, we must acknowledge the powerful role
we as men have in shaping our families. Research shows
again and again that men have a powerful influence on
the faith life of families, on the self-image of our children,
and on the well-being of every one of our immediate and
extended family relations, particularly our partner for
life. If men take a positive, active role in leading their
families—from prayer and church attendance to fun and
games to community involvement—their families will
thrive.

Passage From Scripture

Go home to your family and announce to them
all that the Lord in his pity has done for you.

—Mark 5:19b

Food for Thought

The family in the modern world, as much as
and perhaps more than any other institution,
has been beset by the many profound and rapid
changes that have affected society and culture.
Many families are living this situation in fidelity
to those values that constitute the foundation of
the institution of the family. Others have become
uncertain and bewildered over their role or even
doubtful and almost unaware of the ultimate
meaning and truth of conjugal and family life.
Finally, there are others who are hindered by
various situations of injustice in the realization
of their fundamental rights.

—Pope John Paul II, *Familiaris Consortio*

Discussion and Journaling *(as group or in pairs; spread over two meetings)*

1. As central as your family is to you, many of the
   men in your faith group may not know much
   about your family situation. Take a few minutes to
   describe your immediate family and extended family. Anyone causing headaches or a sleepless night
   or two? Anyone need the prayers of the group? We
   know that your own family members are angels at
   heart, but even angels need our prayers from time
   to time. Share as much as you feel comfortable sharing, knowing that everything shared in the group is
   strictly confidential.

2. Take a moment to do some quiet journaling or thinking. Do you have an image of the ideal family? Describe it. How much does faith enter into this ideal? Now, reflect on how your immediate or extended family reflects (or doesn't) this ideal. What role can you play to change these dynamics, including your family faith life, for the better? You may share your thoughts in pairs or with the group as a whole.

3. Reference the text presented above in Food for Thought. Do you believe that families are under significant stress? In what ways? How can they survive and even flourish in these changing times? If you were able to offer your own pastoral statement on the family, what suggestions would you make to others?

4. Discuss tools that you have tried in your own home, or heard about others using, to bring the family both closer together and into a deeper relationship with Christ. We can learn much from each other.

Exercise

Go around the room and describe a typical dinner scene at home. For those with children at home, don't be afraid to embellish. For those whose children have left the nest, don't be afraid to be realistic. You may well find that one group is jealous of the other. More fundamentally, is everyone present and accounted for at meal time, including you (or are you often absent)? Is there a prayer? Is there mutual respect? Does everyone get a chance to talk, including Dad? If the group is ambitious, try some role-playing or a bit of acting out, just like your children! Are you happy with the way these meals progress? If not, why not—and what might you do to make changes for the better? As the male head of the household, you have an opportunity to make a major impact on this critical family time.

Journal Notes

Additional Reading

The Seven Habits of Highly Effective Families by Stephen R. Covey

The Hidden Value of a Man by Gary Smalley and John Trent

Parenting Your Teens with T.L.C. by Patt and Steve Saso

2.

FAMILY IN SCRIPTURE

For one meeting

Objective: *To delve into scripture for inspiration and guidance as we help lead our families.*

This session is inspired by the imagery surrounding the Feast of the Holy Family, which is celebrated during the Christmas Season, but the meeting may be used at any time of year.

Preparation

To prepare for this session, select a passage from scripture that has special meaning to you as head of a family.

Opening Prayer

Dear Lord, we look to your word to find wisdom
in guiding our families.
We pray that you hear our prayers for loved
ones
and that you guide us in guiding them to your
holy light.
We ask this in your name, O Lord.
Amen.

Humor

The place of the father in the modern suburban
family is a very small one, particularly if he plays
golf.

—Bertrand Russell

Guidance

Scripture is full of examples of men who face choices between right and wrong. Daniel, Job, Jesus, and many others stick by God in the face of enormous pressure. Do they get a hearty pat on the back for their effort? Not so much. More often than not, they appear to be punished for their troubles. To add insult to their injuries, these men often do not even get to see the fruits of their labors. Imagine Moses never getting to see the Promised Land, or the early Christians struggling against mighty odds. Instead, they must rely on faith, and not much more. We, as men, must do the same, particularly with our families.

Our old friend Joseph likely had expectations for his young family. He probably wanted a simple life with a lovely wife and, if God willed it, children to support the family and to extend his own legacy into the future. Well, things don't go quite as planned. They rarely do. Joseph hears shocking news that his fiancée is with child. He is likely reconsidering the whole arrangement when an angel of the Lord intervenes. With only vague instructions, Joseph takes his bride to Nazareth and then again into Egypt to start a new life. And then we hardly hear from him again. Doesn't seem fair, does it?

But it does seem right. And that, precisely, is the point. Leading a family is never easy, but it *is* about doing the right thing for them. We must ask for God's guidance to always do the right thing—whether that is focusing on our kids as much as our customers or leading them in faith.

Passage From Scripture

This saying is trustworthy: whoever aspires to the office of overseer desires a noble task.

Therefore, a bishop must be irreproachable, married only once, temperate, self-controlled, decent, hospitable, able to teach,

not a drunkard, not aggressive, but gentle, not contentious, not a lover of money.

He must manage his own household well, keeping his children under control with perfect dignity;

for if a man does not know how to manage his own household, how can he take care of the church of God?

—1 Timothy 3:1–5

Food for Thought

When we were kids, we complained about going to church. We said, "We're not getting anything out of it." Our dad stopped us right there and said, "You're not supposed to get anything. You go to church to give—to give thanks to God." Now I tell my kids the same thing.

—Michael Gallagher, Boys of Breakfast group

Discussion and Journaling *(as group or in pairs)*

1. From Abraham and his son to Christ's parable of the Prodigal Son, there are dozens of Bible stories about the strain and holiness of family life. Share those that are most meaningful to you with a partner or with the group. Discuss how this passage has touched you in the past or helps to guide you for the future.

2. "So, how's the family?" We are asked this question many times a month. Often, the answer is "fine." Rarely, however, are we asked about the spiritual life of the family. Now's your chance. Take time to

discuss the role that God and church actually do, and potentially could, play in family life.

3. What are ways in which your family takes time to celebrate its faith—truly celebrate it? Be sure to include the simple times together, the unexpected times—not just trips to church!

Exercise *(Ask a member of the group to read the following passage)*

The Feast of the Holy Family is a special celebration to glorify the family of Jesus, Mary, and Joseph and to honor the unique bond of families everywhere. Perhaps not coincidentally, this feast occurs during one of the most chaotic times in a family's calendar: the Sunday between Christmas and New Year's. At this time, most of us are still recovering from the stirring chaos of Christmas and trying to catch our second wind before the beginning of another calendar year. We are, in a word, spent.

The Feast of the Holy Family is born out of a period of what was likely chaos and family distress. Mary and Joseph have just traveled many days to give birth to their new son. Do they get to rest and enjoy the moment? Not for long. Soon after being visited by the Magi, an angel tells Joseph to pack up his family and head to Egypt where they get the privilege of living in exile for many years (Mt 2:13–15). Now how's that for a first Christmas present?

As a group or in pairs, discuss how you imagine that Joseph felt during this time. Did he feel in control of his family, as a father who "knows best"? Or was he, like many men, feeling that he was doing the best he could with the limited resources God had granted him? We recognize the holiness in Joseph's family, as we should in our own. Share your thoughts concerning the holiness you see in your spouse, your children, and in your wider family. Do you ask God's help in guiding them? For it is this inherent holiness, residing in all our families, that we hope to nurture.

Journal Notes

Additional Reading

Raising Faithful Kids in a Fast-Paced World by Dr. Paul Faulkner

Peacemaking for Families by Ken Sande and Tom Raabe

3.

FAITH IN OUR CHILDREN

For two meetings

Objective: *To embrace the role that we have, as fathers, in laying the foundation for a meaningful life in Christ for our children.*

Regardless of the age of our children, be they toddlers or family men of their own, we can play a vital role in how they approach and communicate with God and learn to keep God as their own true north.

Preparation

Prepare for the first meeting by bringing photos of your kids. Also, the leader should make copies of the true north image we used in "Finding True North," beginning on page 7).

Opening Prayer

Father, give us the understanding, the patience, and the desire
to learn to be better fathers.
Help us overcome our daily frustrations with parenthood
and appreciate the amazing gift of watching our children grow.
Just as we, your children, are sometimes led astray,

help us always empathize with our own children and show them the way.
Amen.

Humor

The best way to keep children at home is to make the home atmosphere pleasant—and to let the air out of the tires.

—Dorothy Parker

Guidance

Children reveal how God must feel about us. As any parent knows, our children can be stubborn, joyful, gracious, and horrid—sometimes all within the same hour. And we, in turn, will be in love and exasperated with our children, also during that same hour. How, then, are we to guide our progeny when God seems to have trouble enough with his own? Scripture offers a broad range of stories about children, although most don't sit particularly well with the modern world. There are Abraham about to sacrifice his son and young David felling Goliath with a stone. For the most consistently loving images concerning children, we must turn to Jesus. He singles out children to approach him freely and he reminds his adult followers to be more like them, "for the kingdom of God belongs to such as these" (Mk 10:14). Now this is a man who clearly loves children. What can we learn from him?

As Christ serves as a spiritual and moral center in our lives, so we must be for our children. They seek stability, constancy, and surety in us, just as we seek these in God. As Christ suggests, we need to let children be children so that they can live out God's grace in the world and so that we might learn from them. Treating our children as God treats his own is a tall order, particularly when they are screaming on the floor, or screaming down the block in our car. Yet we really have no choice. They are ours, forever, and we are blessed in our obligation to help them grow and thrive.

Passage From Scripture

> Taking a child he placed it in their midst, and putting his arms around it he said to them, "Whoever receives one child such as this in my name, receives me; and whoever receives me, receives not me but the one who sent me."
>
> —Mark 9:36–37

Food for Thought

> A hundred years from now it will not matter what my bank account was, the sort of house I lived in, or the kind of car I drove . . . but the world may be different because I was important in the life of a child.
>
> —Forest Witcraft

Discussion and Journaling *(as group or in pairs, over two meetings)*

1. Spend some time talking about the kids. Yes, it's important—not just for you, but also for the other members to hear. Along with work, men probably spend more time worrying about their kids—regardless of age—than anything else. Go ahead and share your concerns, and your joys. Remember, parenthood loves company.

2. Throughout the Bible, the most salient feature of most every character is whether he or she has children, and how many. They are considered the greatest blessings and, in some cases, the greatest

burdens. Discuss how having children (or not having them) has changed your outlook on life. More specifically, discuss how they have affected your relationship with God. Have they brought you closer? Can you empathize with the joys and the frustrations that God has with his children, including you?

3. Read the following passage from Kahlil Gibran and discuss it in your group.

> *Your children are not your children. They are the sons and daughters of Life's longing for itself. . . . You are the bows from which your children as living arrows are sent forth. The Archer sees the mark upon the path of the infinite, and he bends you with his might that his arrows may go swift and far. Let your bending in the Archer's hand be for gladness; for even as he loves the arrow that flies, so he loves the bow that is stable.*

Do you agree with the sentiment? Do you see God as the Archer in your life and the life of your children? Do you see yourself as the bow? How does this image impact your role as father and as a spiritual guide for your children, regardless of their age?

Exercise *(discuss as group or in pairs)*

Here, we return to the exercise of true north, which was introduced in the second topical section, "Finding True North" of the first chapter. During this meeting and the next, we ask some basic questions: What is true north for our children? Is it the compass point we want? If not, how can we, our spouses, and our children course-correct for a better way?

A group leader should pass out the star images *(see the Preparation note above)* or have group members draw their own.

1. During the first meeting, write at the bottom of the star what you believe is the perceived true north for your children, regardless of their age. In other words, what seems to guide their decision-making? Are they guided by God, TV, peer pressure, family love, grades, money, pizza bribes? You may need a different star for each child. Now, at the top of the star, write what you want their true north to be—closeness with God, self-confidence, commitment to love, etc. Discuss the differences within the group. One point may emerge from your discussions: most of the images at the bottom are concrete, while most of those at the top are ideals. What can we do to help make these ideals more concrete for our children?

2. For this second part, group members will again work with the star image. Each man should write a list of obstacles to a meaningful course correction on the right side of the star. These may range from lack of time with your children to a whole raft of societal pressures. To the left of the star, list things that you believe will help your children find a path to God and self-fulfillment. Here's a hint: at the very top of the list should be you.

Discuss ways that men can be faith leaders for their children. Beyond mealtime prayer and dragging them to church—though these are important—they will see God through you and your relationship with God. Discuss the ways in which we can better convey that relationship, so that our children (regardless of age) can learn to address the obstacles and find the support they need to develop a positive relationship of their own with Christ.

Journal Notes

Additional Reading

Strong Fathers, Strong Daughters by Meg Meeker
How a Man Prays for His Family by John Yates
The Prophet by Kahlil Gibran
The 7 Habits of Highly Effective Families by Stephen R. Covey

FAITH IN OUR PARTNERS

For two meetings

Objective: *To build closer relationships with our spouses or significant others.*

Most people would recommend spending a lifetime on this topic, as it's mighty complicated. But we'll do our best with two meetings. For the first, we focus on rediscovering what lies at the essence of each relationship. In the second, we will talk about what we can do to rebuild and grow it.

Preparation

No preparation is needed for the first meeting. However, if you will be making a group retreat using the outline, "Exploring Our Relationships with Our Significant Others" provided at www.avemariapress.com or at www.faithbalance.com, we recommend holding these meetings prior to the retreat.

For the second session, prepare by reviewing the retreat outline. Whoever will lead the retreat should bring the outline to the meeting to make notes.

Opening Prayer

Lord, we gather today to discuss one of the most precious gifts
you have given us—our life partners.
We look for ways to better understand them
and build stronger relationships with them.

Help us to approach these relationships with the
humility, love,
and caring they deserve
and to embrace what the Holy Spirit wills for
each man in this group
as a leader in growing these relationships.
In your name we pray.
Amen.

Humor

Only two things are necessary to keep one's wife
happy. One is to let her think she is having her
own way, the other is to let her have it.

—Lyndon B. Johnson

Guidance

God scooped up the earth, blew the breath of life on it,
and created Adam, the first human. Most people assume
that Adam is a male and that "Adam" is a proper name.
However, as Rick Gaillardetz points out in his insightful
article "How Men Find God" (St. Anthony Messenger,
August 2000):

> It turns out . . . that in fact "Adam" is simply the
> English transliteration for the Hebrew ha adam. Ha
> adam is itself a wordplay on the word for the earth,
> which is ha adamah. Ha adam means simply "a
> creature made from the earth." Moreover, there is
> nothing in the Hebrew to suggest that this creature
> yet possesses any gender, male or female.

To put it another way, after bringing forth a horde of
creatures to be named by *Ha adam*, God created a new
creature so that his first creation from the soil would not
feel so lonely. This single act, in effect, created two complete human beings. After the two beings were created,

Adam finally referred to himself as a man, *ish*, and to the other as a woman, *ishah*. The implications are profound— we are made truly complete only through our relationship with another. No wonder we call our partners our "better halves."

Now recall, if you can, your courtship—your own coming to completion through relationship with another. As we know, each person's story is unique, yet the power of love to draw one to another is the same in all of us. It is a power to be honored and nourished, because it comes from God. Love is a gift to be given. The challenge is to find the ways, the means, and the time to do the giving in a substantive way, thereby praising God by fully utilizing the power of his gift of love to nurture, to heal, and to change lives.

Passage From Scripture

The man said: "This one, at last, is bone of my bones and flesh of my flesh; This one shall be called 'woman,' for out of 'her man' this one has been taken."

That is why a man leaves his father and mother and clings to his wife, and the two of them become one body.

—Genesis 2:23–24

Food for Thought

All married couples should learn the art of battle as they should learn the art of making love. Good battle is objective and honest—never vicious or cruel. Good battle is healthy and constructive, and brings to a marriage the principle of equal partnership.

—Ann Landers

Discussion and Journaling *(as group or in pairs, over two meetings)*

First Session

1. The story of how you met your spouse or significant other can be both funny and poignant. As men's groups are often built on the stories we share, take a moment to share one of the most important stories in your life—how you met your life partner.

2. When reflecting on how you met, identify what first attracted you to your wife. Features might include her energy, compassion, humor, faith, spirit, or even good cooking skills. In the second session, we will address how we can rediscover and, in some cases, help to rebuild these affections.

Second Session

1. The Bible is a passionate book. Along with stories of human suffering and triumph, there are heartfelt passages about the power of love. Examples include Genesis 29 (Jacob), Psalm 36, and 1 Corinthians 13. Most people would probably not readily see a connection between religion and romance. Yet God gave us romance for a reason—to draw us into closer relationship with another and, thus, to the Holy Spirit, who thrives on relationship. Take time now to discuss the connection between God and romance. You may be surprised by the responses.

2. Discuss the "art of battle," as Ann Landers described it. In your relationship, what are your patterns of fighting? Are these patterns healthy? Is it possible

to change them, if necessary? Share ideas with the group.

3. Take time to discuss the retreat. Review the outline and make comments, suggestions, edits, or whole-sale changes. Try to reach consensus on the overall objective of the retreat. Fundamentally, the retreat should offer a chance for you to focus on criti-cal relationships—the ones with your significant others—so take time to get it right, both for you and for them.

Exercises

First Session

As author Amy Bloom states, "Love at first sight is easy to understand; it's when two people have been look-ing at each other for a lifetime that it becomes a miracle." As any person in a long-term relationship knows, people change. Our environment, family life, illness, work, and a host of met and unmet expectations change us. One avenue to rebuilding relationships or rekindling the passion is to rediscover what brought you together in the first place. Alone with your journal, in pairs, or as a group, reflect on the stories and the personal attributes you shared in the discussion above. Then take a few min-utes to identify ways to rekindle those areas. Examples range from a simple note of appreciation to an evening discussion of what she needs now to make it until tomor-row, and the day after. Presumably, you know her best, so you can consider what approach will work best. But do *something*. Helping your loved one rediscover her passions will help her rediscover you as well.

Second Session

Consider an evening together with your fellow group members and their "better halves." Shock your wives by arranging everything—dinner, flowers, perhaps an evening activity, and don't forget dessert. The event will offer an excellent opportunity to introduce your partners to the group, to help them feel a part of this journey, and the dividends will be significant. Make it as formal or as casual as you like, but make it special. You both deserve it. For this exercise, discuss the details of the dinner—where (restaurant or hosted at home), when (better check calendars and plan well in advance), what (to eat), and who (will arrange for or prepare the food)—are good places to start. You may also consider a simple icebreaker at the outset of the evening and a special prayer for the evening meal.

Journal Notes

Additional Reading

Moments Together for Couples by Dennis and Barbara Rainey

The Five Love Languages by Gary Chapman

Rekindling the Romance by Dennis and Barbara Rainey

Unconditional Love by John Powell

The Twelve Gifts in Marriage by Charlene Costanzo

5.

SUPPORTING OUR FAMILY'S GIFTS

For one or two meetings

Objective: *To use some of the scriptural tools we discussed in the first chapter, "Centering God and Self," to help identify and nurture the gifts and the talents we see in our family members.*

Preparation

To prepare for this meeting, refer to chapter 1, topic 3 and reacquaint yourself with the gifts and the talents that God has provided to us all.

Opening Prayer

Lord, you have blessed us with our families
Help us to consider the unique gifts, talents, and skills of each of our children, and to nourish these just as you have nourished us in our spiritual growth.
We are thankful for the gifts of our family, and ask that you help us to become better fathers.
Teach us to care for these precious gifts.
Amen.

Humor

One of the most effective ways of sharing the feeling of God's daily presence with the family is to have the children ask the blessing for the evening meal. But, of course, many families don't have this custom, which accounts for the puzzlement of a little boy who went to dinner with his parents at the home of an elderly gentleman. After watching the man bow his head and speak in hushed tones, the boy asked his mother, "What did Mr. Bryan say to his plate?"

—Dick Van Dyke

Guidance

Some days, when we look at our families, it seems incredible that we could be related, much less bound to each other for life. "If only the other family members could be more like me," we sometimes think. Well, that's not going to happen, thank God! The trick is to recognize the diversity within our own family and celebrate it. Just as Paul recognizes that we all have different talents, so we can learn to see and cherish these talents in our family members—even when that talent seems to be for losing things, or being late.

One of our earliest advocates for the notion of self-empowerment was Jesus. As the passage from Luke cited below indicates, Jesus does not want people to hide their gifts under a bushel. God placed that light there. To deny it, hide it away, or suppress it under a mountain of outside expectations would be to turn our backs on God's gift. One of our roles and responsibilities in the family is to help our spouses and children realize their particular gifts. Admittedly, it can be hard to appreciate a child's love for play when she or he needs to finish homework or our spouse's social gifts when you just want a quiet evening at home. A useful metaphor is to think of ourselves as family gardeners. In each of us is a desire to ensure that the seed of our family grows. Yet each part of the garden, each family member, needs a distinct amount of care and nourishment, whether that be full sun or partial shade, and watering daily or once a week. One approach does not fit all. The wise gardener will know when to sow and when to reap. The harvest, of course, is our family and, ultimately, our legacy. This meeting (or meetings if you like) is devoted to reinforcing the wisdom and the patience we need, as co-heads of our families, to help that light shine and to help our garden grow.

Passage From Scripture

No one who lights a lamp conceals it with a vessel or sets it under a bed; rather, he places it on a lampstand so that those who enter may see the light.
For there is nothing hidden that will not become visible, and nothing secret that will not be known and come to light.

—Luke 8:16–17

Food for Thought

The only gift is a portion of thyself.

—Ralph Waldo Emerson

Discussion *(as group or in pairs, over one or two meetings to allow each member time to share)*

1. Take time to go through each member of your immediate family and identify his or her core gifts. These may be the gift of laughter, curiosity, boundless energy, or any number of other special attributes. Are these gifts being nurtured in your home? What might you do, as a family leader, to help ensure that these gifts are realized?

2. If you could give each member of your family a
   spiritual, emotional, or mental gift, what would
   that be? The gift of courage, of grace, of trust in
   oneself and in God? As you discuss these items,
   consider the power you have in the family to make
   these gifts a reality in your home. Consider what
   you might do to bring these timeless gifts, which
   don't break easily or run short on batteries, to your
   family members.

Exercise *(discuss as group or in pairs)*

In 1995, Daniel Goleman published *Emotional Intelligence*, a national bestseller that forced people to look
beyond IQ as a standard measurement for intelligence.
He effectively divided a person's personality into four
quadrants: self-awareness, social awareness, self-
management, and relationship management. People tend
to be stronger in one or maybe two of these areas than the
others. These strengths and weaknesses help determine
how we interact within our families and with the world.
Thinking about individual personality traits from this
perspective can also provide an important reminder that
everyone has much to offer, if we have the wisdom to
see the potential in people and the patience to give them
a chance.

On a piece of paper, write out Goleman's four quadrants. In the top two quadrants, put self-awareness
and social awareness, and in the bottom two, self-
management and relationship management. Then write
the names of your family members wherever you think
most appropriate, based on individual strengths. Discuss
your placement and how, as a leader in the family, you
can help nurture and build on these innate gifts.

Journal Notes

Additional Reading

Emotional Intelligence: 10th Anniversary Edition by Daniel
    Goleman
The 7 Habits of Highly Effective Families by Steven R.
    Covey
Gift of Fatherhood by Aaron Hass

FAITH IN OUR FATHERS

For one meeting

Objective: *To examine some parallels between our relationships with our own fathers and with God as father.*

This meeting is not meant to be a therapy session probing the deep mysteries of the father-son relationship; there simply are not enough couches to go around! Rather, this is an opportunity to reflect on a vitally important relationship in our life.

Preparation

No advanced preparation is necessary.

Opening Prayer

Our Father, who art in heaven,
hallowed be your name.
Your kingdom come;
your will be done on earth, as it is in heaven.
Give us this day our daily bread,
and forgive us our trespasses,
as we forgive those who trespass against us,
and lead us not into temptation,
but deliver us from evil.
Amen.

Humor

> By the time a man realizes that maybe his father
> was right, he usually has a son who thinks he's
> wrong.
>
> —Charles Wadsworth

Guidance

A man's relationship with his father is complex, to say the least. We may be bound by love, anger, frustration, and longing—all jumbled up together. In fact, this relationship can seem more complex, and more dynamic, than our relationship with God the Father. Why is this so? And what can we learn from each that may be applied to the other?

The relationship with our birth father is personal and immediate, even if he has been absent for a long time. We would do well to nurture such intimacy with God. On the other hand, the relationship is often so intense that it can become fixed in time. For better or worse, this relationship may be fixed from a long time ago, during that relatively short period of time called our "formative years." Yet, as we have discussed in previous meetings on family, people change. As a result, the dynamics of our relationships should change as well. What if our relationship with God the Father was the same as when we were six, or ten, or fifteen? Our faith would be constrained, even immature. We would fail to see the fullness of God or truly appreciate the role he plays in our lives. If we remained fixed on those times when God did not "deliver" on our prayers, we might not appreciate the full extent of God's wisdom and love.

In this session, we take time to honor our fathers by trying to see them as they are, not who they were or how we want or remember them to be. We honor God the Father as well by reaching out to him as one would a human father. If we allow it, our earthly and heavenly fathers mutually reinforce the deeply personal stake we have, or should have, in both.

Passage From Scripture

When I was a child, I used to talk as a child, think as a child, reason as a child; when I became a man, I put aside childish things.

At present we see indistinctly, as in a mirror, but then face to face. At present I know partially; then I shall know fully, as I am fully known.

—1 Corinthians 13:11–12

Food for Thought

You don't pay back your parents. You can't. The debt you owe them gets collected by your children, who hand it down in turn. It's a sort of entailment. Or if you don't have children of the body, it's left as a debt to your common humanity.

—Lois McMaster Bujold

Discussion *(as group or in pairs)*

1. Describe some positive attributes and some negative attributes of your father. In what way do you feel you are like your father? In what ways have you tried to be different—in your attitude and in your family relationships?

2. Jesus spoke of forgiveness as a virtue. The Father forgives our sins (trespasses), as we are to forgive those who have sinned against us. In pairs or as a whole, discuss the role that forgiveness has played, or how it has been absent, in the relationship with your own father. Where is there room for improvement?

3. Presumably your relationship with God has evolved over time. Compare the relationship you had with God the Father as a child with the one you have now as an adult. What has been gained (appreciation, trust, understanding)? What has been lost (intimacy, trust, wonder)? Discuss how you might take the best of both and fashion a closer relationship with God the Father.

Exercise (*as group or in pairs*)

Imagine that it's Father's Day ten or twenty years from now. Even if your father is absent, write a brief note to him. What would you say? Now write a second note, imagining what you would like your children to say about you. Notice any similarities, or differences? What role does God play? You need not share these notes with the other members of the group, but we encourage you to discuss as much as you feel comfortable sharing. You will likely discover that other men's relationships with their father are as complex and deep-rooted as your own.

Journal Notes

Additional Reading

Fatherhood by Bill Cosby
Gift of Fatherhood by Aaron Hass

Balancing Faith and Work

● ●

Topics

●   ●   ●   ●   ●   ●   ●   ●   ●

1. Faith in the Workplace

2. Defining Mission

3. Finding Purpose at Work

4. Spiritual Leadership

5. Taking Stock

6. Spiritual Legacy Building

7.

FAITH IN THE WORKPLACE

For one or two meetings

Objective: *To better appreciate God's role in the workplace and to better align our own faith lives within and beyond the work environment.*

In later meetings, we explore how some tools and techniques from work can actually be applied to our spiritual life including the mission statement, the planning process, and the development of leadership and communication skills. For those who are retired, this theme is also applicable, as lessons learned from a career of work can have lasting impact on our interactions today. Moreover, retirees have a valuable perspective to share in the true value and significance of work.

Preparation

No advance preparation is needed for this meeting, just a willingness to listen and learn from each other.

Opening Prayer

Lord, thank you for our men's fellowship today.
Help us respectfully find ways to embrace our faith in the workplace,
and seek the Holy Spirit in managing our decisions, relationships,
and leadership style at work
so that they align with who we are in other areas of our lives.

Help us appreciate the diversity of beliefs we
encounter at work
and embrace others in the same manner that
your Son, Jesus would.
We ask this in your name.
Amen.

Humor

By working faithfully eight hours a day, you
may eventually get to be a boss and work twelve
hours a day.

—Robert Frost

Guidance

When many people go to work, they leave their faith
at the door and do so with good reason. Work is largely
about helping your team, however that may be defined,
meet stated objectives. For most work teams, those objectives involve making money in one form or another.
There is usually not much room for God below the bottom line. So many of us tuck the Holy Spirit away, keep
Christ hidden in our hearts, and rip through our contacts
list to make the next customer call. A lucky few have
not felt compelled to hide their faith, but nevertheless
struggle daily with how much of it can be shared in the
workplace. Yet if God is everywhere, then he must be at
work as well.

In India, where Steve has lived and worked, the
business environment is very different from that in the
United States. All beliefs are celebrated. Once a year, the
office will host a Hindu prayer, or puja, to bless the workings of the group. Muslims are encouraged to pray in
special areas during work. And all religious holidays—
Hindu, Muslim, Christian, Buddhist, and Sikh—are at
least acknowledged if not openly celebrated. It is a policy

that does not shrink from the diversity of faith, but rather values God worshipped in many forms.

What can we learn from this approach? Perhaps it is simply that faith is something to be celebrated and shared in all walks of life, including work. Christ calls us into relationship with others for that is where we will find God. The challenge is to seek out those relationships and to share our beliefs in ways that are respectful and welcoming. Our job, if you will, is to find the Holy Spirit in our colleagues and even in our customers so that we might live out God's glory in others as well as in ourselves. We know this is easier said than done. Yet, there are viable options for acknowledging and sharing faith in the context of work and we hope to explore them in the coming meetings.

Passage From Scripture

Only, conduct yourselves in a way worthy of the gospel of Christ, so that, whether I come and see you or am absent, I may hear news of you, that you are standing firm in one spirit, with one mind struggling together for the faith of the gospel.

—Philippians 1:27

Food for Thought

I know God will not give me anything I can't handle. I just wish that He didn't trust me so much.

—Mother Teresa of Calcutta

Discussion and Journaling *(as group or in pairs, may be spread over two meetings)*

1. We spend (or spent if retired) many if not most of our waking hours involved with work. As we begin

to look at faith in the workplace, describe your workplace to the others in the group. Do you spend more time with people or with your computer? How is the commute? Describe your colleagues. How's the coffee? No value judgments (except maybe for the coffee); just provide a sense of how you spend (or spent) your days so that the other men in the group have a clearer picture for directing their prayers.

2. For any who are retired in the group, share your perspective on the good, bad, and ugly of your days in the workplace. Is there anything you would have done differently or more often? Many men lack perspective when it comes to their work experience, so this is a nice opportunity to hear from someone who has literally "been there, and done that." For those still working, try to imagine your retirement day. How are you likely to look back on your years of toil? Is there time for a course correction now?

3. Do you experience or perceive any tension or conflict between your faith and your work? If so, how is this manifested? Are you able to integrate your faith and work? If so, how do you do this? If not, why not? Share your thoughts and lessons learned with others. You can tie this into the exercise discussion below.

Exercise

As a group or in pairs, discuss your experience in expressing faith in the workplace. One low-risk technique for identifying other men and women of faith in the workplace is to drop simple references to church or prayer into casual conversations. For example, mention your men's faith group in the context of a talk about how you spent the weekend, or about your morning commute, etc. Your work colleagues will notice, guaranteed, and can choose to pursue the subject or not. Brainstorm other ways to explore and incorporate faith in the workplace.

As a suggested exercise, if you are comfortable, try role-playing in pairs to test out how conversations like the ones mentioned above might go in reality.

Journal Notes

Additional Reading

Work With Meaning, Work With Joy by Pat McHenry Sullivan

Believers in Business by Laura L. Nash

God Is My CEO by Larry Julian

2.

DEFINING MISSION

For two meetings

Objective: *To develop our own personal mission statements, which are inspired by Christ's mission for us.*

Many of us are familiar with organizational mission statements. At their best, mission statements help guide and reinforce a collective vision for the future. At their worst, they are meaningless documents that confuse more than inspire. Our personal mission in life will likely evolve over time, but should always reflect our core values and provide some level of inspiration for the future.

Preparation

Prior to the first meeting, group members should consider what constitutes a meaningful mission statement. If anyone doesn't have experience with mission statements, he might look into what they generally contain and how organizations utilize them.

Opening Prayer

Lord, we recognize that you have created
all that we have, see, and do in our lives.
Your greatest hope for us is that we each live a
life of purpose
with what we've been given.
You have blessed us with unique gifts and talents.
You have brought special people and relationships into our lives.

We pray that you help each of us recognize our
mission in life
as individuals and collectively.
Help us use this men's fellowship time wisely
as a means for highlighting a more purposeful
life.
In your name we pray.
Amen.

Humor

God put me on Earth to accomplish a certain
number of things. Right now I'm so far behind I
will never die!

—Bill Watterson

Guidance

Christ is clear about our mission. During his final
meal with the disciples in John's gospel he says, "I give
you a new commandment: love one another. As I have
loved you, so you also should love one another" (Jn
13:34). Paul, who is big on missions, is also clear. "Serve
one another through love" (Gal 5:13). Meanwhile, in our
typical workday, we are presented with many, often less
inspiring, missions. To better serve one's customers, to
meet quota, to find a parking space. How do we balance
the lofty missions from heaven with the more mundane
ones on earth?

It is important to remember that God has given us life
and our unique gifts for a very good reason. He wants
us to use them to bring the Good News of salvation to
our world. In these two meetings, we take time to write
our own mission statements, ones that integrate the calls
of discipleship with the life and the gifts we are given.
An honest, meaningful mission statement can serve as a

touchstone for using these gifts, as a regular reminder to live out God's vision for us in the world.

We will bring together previous discussions on finding God and our own True North as well as a better appreciation of our God-given talents, our self-worth, and our true significance in the world. Begin with a prayer and reflect on Christ's call to "seek first the kingdom (of God) and his righteousness, and all these things will be given you besides" (Mt 6:33).

Passage From Scripture

Many are the plans in a man's heart, but it is the decision of the LORD that endures.

—Proverbs 19:21

Food for Thought

What I really lack is to be clear in my mind what I am to do, not what I am to know. . . . The thing is to understand myself, to see what God really wishes me to do . . . to find the idea for which I can live and die.

—Soren Kierkegaard

Discussion *(as group or in pairs)*

First Meeting

What constitutes a meaningful mission statement? What separates a lasting statement from one that is empty? If possible, share the mission statement from your own workplace (or the heart of it anyway). Does it motivate people or not? Why?

Exercise

Take several minutes to draft a short personal/life mission statement, of no more than one to three sentences. It need not be perfect, or even complete, because our missions will naturally evolve over time just as our understanding of God will evolve and mature over time. When you have finished, or at least scratched out some ideas, share with a partner or with the group. No judgments please; this is personal and confidential.

Before the next meeting, revise and sharpen your mission statement. Be sure to pray and let God into your revisions.

Second Meeting

1. Discuss what elements you would expect in a meaningful personal mission statement. What role does God play in your definition? What role does family have? How about our personal aspirations? Discuss how a personal mission statement should both reflect and reinforce what is truly important to you.

2. Share your revised mission statements, which you hopefully have considered between meetings. Go around the room and discuss the statements, making helpful suggestions when appropriate.

Exercise

When the group feels ready, we recommend developing accountability partners, or teams. Take time to identify teams of two to four people and then split up for several minutes of discussion. Agree among yourselves about how you want to communicate between meetings, such as occasional check-in, remembrance in prayer, or an occasional lunch. The goal is to help each other keep these mission statements alive in our hearts and minds.

Journal Notes

Additional Reading

The Purpose-Driven Life by Rick Warren
The 7 Habits of Highly Effective People by Stephen R. Covey
From Success to Significance by Lloyd Reeb

3.

FINDING PURPOSE
AT WORK

For one or two meetings

Objective: *To remind ourselves of the blessings of labor and the pride we can take in good works; to reflect on colleagues who help us in our labors, take time to honor and pray for them.*

Preparation

Bring a biblical or historical reference to a person whose work you admire. Examples include the Wisdom of Solomon, the leadership of David, and the "marketing and communications" success of Paul. You will need at least one bible on hand for the fourth discussion question.

Opening Prayer

Lord, we ask that you bless us today
with the ability to thoughtfully review our jobs
and careers
and the role they play in our lives.
Help us to distinguish what is important, meaningful, and significant
in the grand scheme of things, to ourselves, and
you, Lord.
Remind us that our purpose on earth
is to enjoy the fruit of our labor on behalf of your
kingdom.
Amen.

Humor

> I don't want to achieve immortality through my work. . . . I want to achieve it through not dying.

> —Woody Allen

Guidance

In the Bible are many references to the value of good works. The well-ploughed field and fruits of a good harvest are heavenly rewards for earthly labor. Even in the Garden of Eden, God expected good works: "The LORD God then took the man and settled him in the garden of Eden, to cultivate and care for it" (Gn 2:15). Jesus uses many parables that involve work and the rewards, however intangible, that we may receive from it. Moreover, God needs laborers, as many as possible, to work the fields of faith and to tend his garden on earth. "Then he said to his disciples, 'The harvest is abundant but the laborers are few; so ask the master of the harvest to send out laborers for his harvest'" (Mt 9:37–38).

Throughout these passages, is a common, unspoken theme we would do well to acknowledge: the value of having pride in our work. God expects us to do our best in whatever circumstances we may find ourselves, whether we are living in a beautiful garden or laboring in painful toil outside the garden walls (Gn 3:17). While we may not be rewarded as we might like or achieve all we had planned, God assuredly delights in our efforts because he wants us to use the gifts we have been given. "For the Son of Man will come with his angels in his Father's glory, and then he will repay everyone according to his conduct" (Mt 16:27).

Passage From Scripture

One thing God has said; two things I have heard:
Power belongs to God;
so too, Lord, does kindness, And you render to
each of us according to our deeds.

— Psalm 62:12–13

Food for Thought

Pray as if everything depended upon God and
work as if everything depended upon man.

— Francis Cardinal Spellman

Discussion and Journaling *(as group or in pairs, may be spread over two meetings)*

1. Share the story of a biblical or historical figure whose work you admire. Discuss what qualities you admire most in that person. Recall an earlier meeting on the distinction between success and significance. What makes this person's success of lasting significance?

2. Discuss the underlying purpose of your work. Look beyond the typical organizational objectives to meet payroll or your monthly quota. Does the quality of your work, or your demeanor, have an impact on your colleagues and customers and, ultimately, on your own sense of self-worth? How do these affect your sense of purpose at work?

3. Discuss the impact of colleagues on your work, now and in the past. For those who have been lucky enough to find mentors at work, share those stories with others.

4. Read the Parable of the Talents (Mt 25:14–30). Discuss Christ's underlying message about the role of work in our lives. How are we to use what has been entrusted to us?

Exercise *(discuss as group or in pairs)*

In your journal, in pairs, or with the whole group, construct a memo to yourself regarding your purpose at work. Use bullet points if you like. Reflect on our reading and discussion questions regarding the importance of taking pride in our work as well as the impact of our work on others. If you can, include at least two bullet items concerning how we might approach work differently in order to raise the level of our pride and our impact on others. If you prefer, put it on a sticky note and stick it to your wallet, to help you remember reasons—besides money—why we work so much. Share your findings with the group; their stories may change your own perspective.

Journal Notes

Additional Reading

God Is Work by Ken Eldred
The Path by Laurie Beth Jones
Conscious Business by Fred Kofman

SPIRITUAL LEADERSHIP

For one or two meetings

Objective: *To explore together the qualities of spiritual leadership at work, in our families, and in our community.*

True leadership is a rare quality, yet God has provided each of us with qualities to lead his message into the world.

Preparation

Come ready to discuss leaders and leadership styles you admire. The leader may want to make copies of the star image from chapter 1, topic 2 for use with the exercise.

Opening Prayer

Lord, we know that you already consider us
leaders in our community,
through the fellowship that we have developed
and the example we are setting in this men's
faith group.
Help us grow our spiritual leadership in our
homes,
our community, and at work.
Make us true disciples of Jesus by following his
spiritual leadership.
We ask that you bless us

in the name of the Father, the Son, and the Holy
Spirit.
Amen.

Humor

You do not lead by hitting people over the
head—that's assault, not leadership.

—Dwight D. Eisenhower

Guidance

As we progress in our career and in the world, most
of us will assume greater leadership positions. Retirement then provides the gift of time, which we can use to
share our leadership skills and wisdom with others. We
may now, or in the near future, find ourselves running an
organization, managing a small team of people, or leading committees in the community. In each case, we have
an opportunity to influence people in how they live and
work. We also have a responsibility to be good stewards
of all with which we have been entrusted.

As men of God, we have an additional role to play. We
serve as models to others for how Christ can and should
be manifested here on earth. To draw a lesson from the
business world, we can think of ourselves as marketing
executives for Christ. Just as the advertising world uses
"word of mouth" marketing, you too can we create a
"viral marketing network" that is truly self-perpetuating
through evangelization. Living our faith as leaders in
the community announces the Good News to all those
around us. This is spiritual leadership. People see the
light and start talking, if not to others then at least to
themselves, and word of mouth marketing has begun. As
the Food for Thought quote below suggests, we do not
always need words to convey the message of Christ. Our
leadership style alone is message enough. The degree to

which we show compassion and confidence, passion and purpose—just as Christ did with his followers—will ultimately determine our effectiveness as a Christian leader.

Passage From Scripture

Only, conduct yourselves in a way worthy of the gospel of Christ, so that, whether I come and see you or am absent, I may hear news of you, that you are standing firm in one spirit, with one mind struggling together for the faith of the gospel.

—Philippians 1:27

Food for Thought

Preach the gospel at all times. Use words if necessary.

—St. Francis of Assisi

Discussion *(as group or in pairs)*

1. Identify current or past leaders you admire. What are the leadership qualities you admire most? Why are/were they effective?

2. Was Christ a traditional leader? How would he fare in the workplace today? What aspects of his leadership style can we adapt to our work place? To our attempts at evangelization?

3. Try to put into your own words what it means to be a spiritual leader? Are you currently practicing spiritual leadership at work? In the community? At home? If not, why not?

Exercise *(after some journaling, discuss as group or in pairs)*

We can apply the principle of a spiritual true north to leadership and decision-making. With respect to your own decision-making and leadership, what is true north? What are your guiding principles when making decisions—efficiency, integrity, faith? Now, what are the obstacles you face in implementing the leadership style you would like to have? What can you do to reinforce that leadership, to keep you focused on your true north? Write these elements in your journal and discuss them with your peers.

Alternate Exercise *(perhaps at a second meeting)*

Read a Bible passage in which Jesus shows his leadership style. Some examples to get you going are: Jesus using parables, Jesus at the Passover table, or Jesus washing the feet of his disciples. Then have the group discuss how each person can be more Christ-like in their leadership style at work or home.

Journal Notes

Additional Reading:

Spiritual Leadership by Henry and Richard Blackaby
God Is My CEO by Larry Julian
Courageous Leadership by Bill Hybels
Jesus on Leadership by C. Gene Wilkes
The Management Methods of Jesus by Bob Briner

5.

TAKING STOCK

For one to three meetings

Objective: *To consider the many facets of our rich lives, including our never-ending quest to balance family, work, faith, and the time to actually enjoy God's bounty on earth.*

If we stop to take stock of all we have worked for, while creating a renewed vision for all we would still like to become, we can find more meaning in our day-to-day triumphs and challenges. Finding balance in life is, in many respects, simply about keeping things in perspective.

Preparation

Review some of the notes or discussion questions from chapter 1, "Centering God and Self." We will return to some of the same messages here.

Opening Prayer

Lord, we are very thankful
for the rich lives you have granted us thus far,
and for the fellowship we have in this group.
We ask today that you help us review our own lives
and evaluate them in a spirit of charity.
Help us to determine whether the lives we are living today
put us on the trajectory we wish to be on for eternity.

Help us consider ways we can alter our current paths
in order to better do your bidding.
We pray in your name.
Amen.

Humor

Experience is the name everyone gives to their mistakes.

—Oscar Wilde

Guidance

Whereas women may think of life as seasonal, with events and relationships recurring in cycles over time, men tend to think more linearly. To us, life may be more like a river. It begins as a small stream, builds in size as we grow, and twists and turns toward eventual union with God. Along the way, we experience love and loss, triumph and tragedy. From time to time, we look backward and forward at the long and winding river of our lives and hope that we feel a sense of peace and satisfaction in what we see.

There are other analogies, of course. In his book *Half-time*, Bob Buford sees life as a football game. The game, like life, has a beginning, an end, and a period called "halftime" that allows us to reflect on and prepare for the second phase of our life. During this second phase, men may begin to think about their significance and legacy more than their annual accomplishments. They may realize there are new priorities in life, such as spending time with family or simply appreciating more of what life has to offer. This is appropriate. What some people call a personal crisis is simply God's inner call to take stock of life. We ignore this call at our own risk. So, for the next session or two, we will heed this call and reflect on where we've come from and where we'd like to go.

Passage From Scripture

There is an appointed time for everything, and a time for every affair under the heavens.

A time to be born, and a time to die; a time to plant, and a time to uproot the plant.

A time to kill, and a time to heal; a time to tear down, and a time to build.

A time to weep, and a time to laugh; a time to mourn, and a time to dance.

A time to scatter stones, and a time to gather them; a time to embrace, and a time to be far from embraces.

A time to seek, and a time to lose; a time to keep, and a time to cast away.

A time to rend, and a time to sew; a time to be silent, and a time to speak.

A time to love, and a time to hate; a time of war, and a time of peace.

What advantage has the worker from his toil?

I have considered the task which God has appointed for men to be busied about.

He has made everything appropriate to its time, and has put the timeless into their hearts, without men's ever discovering, from beginning to end, the work which God has done.

I recognized that there is nothing better than to be glad and to do well during life.

For every man, moreover, to eat and drink and enjoy the fruit of all his labor is a gift of God.

I recognized that whatever God does will endure forever; there is no adding to it, or taking from it. Thus has God done that he may be revered.

—Ecclesiastes 3:1–14

Food for Thought

The longest journey is the journey inward.

—Dag Hammarskjöld

Discussion *(as group or in pairs)*

1. Write down in your journal, or discuss as a group, the biggest events in your life to date. Consider how one key event or decision helps determine the next event; like a pebble dropped into a pool, creating ripples that move out in unexpected ways. Try to see the patterns—a meeting at school that leads to a marriage, a job that leads to a move, or a chance encounter with someone that shapes an important decision. What role do you believe God has played in these changes? Do you typically pray before a big decision? Have the ripple effects of any decision affected how you make decisions? Do you see these effects as immobilizing or energizing, or a bit of both?

2. Next, write down in your journal, or discuss in pairs, some regrets that you have so far in your life. If you have no regrets, then congratulations are in order. Consider a road not taken—a move, a job change, an airplane pilot's license—and the ripple effects that might have had. Do you feel that Christ was a part of these decisions as well?

Exercise *(may take two or three meetings)*

Consider the multiple roles and responsibilities we have in our lives. You are likely a worker bee and a family man; a leader and a follower; a faithful servant and an occasional sinner. In your journal or as a group, write in one column the various titles you hold in life—husband, father, brother, son, salesman, teacher, accountant, coach, etc. In a middle column, write the roles you play in fulfilling these responsibilities—leader, follower, helper, provider, etc. Now, in a third column, write your perceived purposes in serving these roles—to make money, create a legacy, share love, spread the Word of God. Take stock of these connections. Do the titles and the responsibilities you hold support what you hope to achieve? If not, why not? What might you do, with God's help, to ensure a stronger connection between what you actually do and how you do it, as well as what you hope to achieve?

Journal Notes

Additional Reading

Halftime by Bob Buford
Game Plan by Bob Buford
Finishing Well by Bob Buford
From Success to Significance by Lloyd Reeb
The Purpose-Driven Life by Rick Warren

6.

SPIRITUAL LEGACY BUILDING

Objective: *To expand our vision from our impact at work to the legacy of our lives.*

This is a transitional topic into the next chapter, "Growing Our Faith in the World."

Preparation

Reflect on your heritage and the history of your ancestors and come prepared to share these stories with the group. We will discuss how you, in turn, will leave a legacy for generations to come. Also, bring the mission statement that you developed in the meetings on Defining Mission.

Opening Prayer

Lord, today as we talk among brothers,
we ask that you reveal to us something about our
spiritual calling in life.
Help us look into our hearts to better understand
the legacy
we wish to leave here on earth.
We know that you have a plan for each of us, and
we wish to follow it.
Fill us with the Holy Spirit to allow each of us to
hear our calling and your bidding.
In your name we pray.
Amen.

Humor

If you want to make God laugh, tell him your plans.

—Folk proverb

Guidance

We are the product of many generations. Whether we know of them or not, our forefathers and foremothers bequeathed to us their legacy. We may have inherited our great uncle's tenacity or the gleam in a distant cousin's eye. We were born to a place that resulted from their individual choices, a hundred decisions made across a dozen generations. And now, the decisions we make will have an impact on generations to come. We will not know these people, but they are our legacy. Decisions like how we treat our children, how we conduct ourselves at work, and where we will retire are the seeds of our unfolding legacy. God plays a role, of course, in whether these seeds bear lasting fruit. Only God can know the full impact of our decisions. Still, we do make choices every day concerning the company we keep and how we treat them, or the work we do and the pride we take in doing it. Ultimately, we determine the condition of the seeds of our legacies.

What Jesus teaches in Matthew's Gospel can easily be applied to our legacies:

> By their fruits you will know them. Do people pick grapes from thorn bushes, or figs from thistles?
> Just so, every good tree bears good fruit, and a rotten tree bears bad fruit.
> A good tree cannot bear bad fruit, nor can a rotten tree bear good fruit.

Every tree that does not bear good fruit will be
cut down and thrown into the fire.
So by their fruits you will know them.

—Matthew 7:16–20

The key to remember is that, whether we like it or not,
our presence on earth does leave a legacy for the future.
The good news is that we can begin shaping our legacies
today.

Passage From Scripture

I have set before you life and death, the blessing
and the curse. Choose life, then, that you and
your descendants may live, by loving the LORD,
your God, heeding his voice, and holding fast to
him. For that will mean life for you, a long life
for you to live on the land which the LORD swore
he would give to your fathers Abraham, Isaac,
and Jacob.

—Deuteronomy 30:19–20

Food for Thought

God's call is for you to be his loyal friend, for
whatever purpose he has for your life.

—Oswald Chambers

Discussion *(as group or in pairs)*

1. Share your family history. Where did your ancestors come from and how did they arrive in America? What did they do after they arrived? Do you
   think they would consider their lives 'successful'?

2. The Merriam-Webster dictionary (2007), defines
   legacy as: "a gift by will especially of money or
   other personal property" or "something transmit-
   ted by or received from an ancestor or predecessor

or from the past." How does creating a legacy factor into your life? Do you care if you leave a legacy? If so, for whom are you trying to leave a legacy? Why do you suppose it is important for you to do so?

3. If leaving a legacy is not important to you, why not? What is more important to you?

Exercise

Remember your mission statements? They can help prioritize where we want to go and the impact we hope to have on the future. In pairs or with the group as a whole, discuss your statement in the context of your potential legacy. Does it reinforce the choice of life, as Deuteronomy states, so that "you and your descendants my live, by loving the LORD, your God"?

Discuss what choosing life truly means. This is a critical question that shapes all people of faith, for God wants us to live out his Word in the world. After discussion, return to your statement to discern how best to align your current mission with the life you want to lead and the legacy you hope to leave. Offer prayers and suggestions for each other, so that we may all choose life.

Journal Notes

Additional Reading

A Travel Guide To Heaven by Anthony DeStefano
The 8th Habit by Stephen R. Covey
Halftime by Bob Buford
Your Unforgettable Life by Jennifer Schuchmann and Craig
  Chapin

Growing Faith in the World

Topics

1. Individual Service
2. Appreciating Other Faiths
3. Spiritual Community Leadership
4. Wealth and Charity
5. Group Community Service

7.

INDIVIDUAL SERVICE

For three meetings

Objective: *To reflect on our God-given talents and discuss how we can apply them 1) in the Church, 2) in the local community, and 3) in the wider world.*

We recommend devoting a session to each of these opportunities, in that order. The proposed discussion questions and exercise are designed to encourage members to focus on these areas of need and to identify ways to apply our talents in addressing these needs. Such service sows the seeds for our true legacy.

Preparation

Return to the notes from chapter 1, topic 3 concerning spiritual gifts and talents. Bring your list to the meetings and be prepared to discuss how your gifts and talents might be applied for the greater glory of God. If you do not have this list, review this earlier session and start fresh. Gifts may include talking or listening, leading or supporting, creating or fixing, and on and on.

Opening Prayer

Lord, in Proverbs 11, you say to us that
"One [who] is lavish yet grows still richer;
another is too sparing, yet is the poorer."
We open our hearts today to ask what we can do
in this larger world,

how can we contribute our unique gifts and talents that come from you?
Teach us how we can contribute something back for all that you have given us.
In your name we pray.
Amen.

Humor

When you have told anyone you have left him a legacy the only decent thing to do is to die at once.

—Samuel Butler

Guidance

In the session on spiritual gifts in chapter 1, topic 3, we tried to identify the God-given talents that we possess and began to think how we might be able to use them. Beyond family, work, and weekly Mass is a wider world that could use a little help. In baptism we are called to serve that world, to bring it the Good News of salvation to people in need. It's important to remember that community involvement is not a lifetime commitment. Many people avoid getting involved because they're afraid of such commitments, and that is a shame. This is not a wedding. Try helping just one day at a soup kitchen or with a clothing drive; or sign up for a simple ministry at church. There is a need for every talent and, if we all step forward, a talent for every need. The only recommendation we would make is to *make your participation personal*. We are called to Christ through relationships and through him into service in the same way. Only by meeting people who are in need of the gifts we have to share do we come to know and love them, as the life of discipleship requires of us. Don't be shy—your legacy waits!

Passage From Scripture

What good is it, my brothers, if someone says he has faith but does not have works? Can that faith save him? If a brother or sister has nothing to wear and has no food for the day, and one of you says to them, "Go in peace, keep warm, and eat well," but you do not give them the necessities of the body, what good is it? So also faith of itself, if it does not have works, is dead.

—James 2:14–17

Food for Thought

The Christian ideal has not been tried and found wanting; it has been found difficult and left untried.

—G.K. Chesterton

Discussion and Journaling *(as group or in pairs)*

1. What has been your experience with respect to helping out at church or in the community? Positive or negative? Were your talents appropriately used? What can you learn from your experience to make your next opportunity for involvement more meaningful, both for you and the people you would like to help?

2. It is said that it's easier to get a social activist to convert to Christianity than it is to get many Christians to become actively involved in the community. Why is this so? What could be done to make this transition easier?

Exercise *(discuss as group or in pairs)*

First Meeting

Have the group generate a list of Church ministries in which lay people participate. List these on a wide piece of paper. Another option is to have the group leader list the ministries available at your local parish or parishes and provide this to group members. A list of volunteer ministries is available on many parish websites. The possibilities are many: parish or finance council member; greeter or usher for liturgies; leader of Children's Liturgy of the Word; care of the sick, bereavement, or family life ministries; catechist; building and grounds maintenance—to name a few. Now, write your name and your talent next to a ministry that seems to fit your time, talent, and interests. This is *not* a commitment, only a mark for future consideration and an indication that you do, indeed, have much to offer.

Second Meeting

As a group, brainstorm local community activities that are available. To help focus the discussion, the group leader or a designated member should go to the Web and print out a range of community organizations that could use part-time volunteers. Many local government websites provide links to volunteer opportunities. Again, mark your talents and consider getting involved. If you don't have time, it's always fun to volunteer other family members. You can live vicariously through them!

Third Meeting

Now, we take on the world. In the Additional Reading section below, we list a range of websites that have information about national and international organizations that would be happy to have your help. Again, have a group member print out information on some of these organizations and discuss what they do. In this case, you don't need to volunteer—learning is enough at this point. But if you do feel called to service, feel free to contact these or other organizations directly.

Journal Notes

Additional Reading

A Concise Guide to Catholic Social Teaching by Kevin E. McKenna

The Power of Generosity by Dave Toycen

Parish websites, for volunteer ministry opportunities:

Catholic Relief Services, www.crs.org, the official international relief and development agency of the U.S. Catholic community.

Catholic Charities USA, www.catholiccharitiesusa.org, a member network of local agencies providing help and creating hope for people of all faiths.

Habitat for Humanity, www.habitat.org, a nonprofit, ecumenical Christian housing ministry.

Guidestar, www.guidestar.org, provides summaries and rankings of non-profits throughout the United States.

Idealist, www.idealist.org, networking site for service opportunities worldwide.

Opportunity International, www.opportunity.org, a micro-finance institution.

Kiva, www.kiva.org, lending projects around the world.

Community to People, www.c2people.org, makes no-interest micro-bridge loans.

2.

APPRECIATING
OTHER FAITHS

(for several meetings)

Objective: *To better understand and appreciate faith traditions other than our own.*

In order to truly understand our own religion, it is good to understand the religions of others. We recommend spending a full meeting on each of the world's major religions, or as many as you can manage. In addition to exploring other Christian churches, you might include Buddhism, Hinduism, Islam, Judaism, and Sikhism.

Preparation

Ask for volunteers, or assign one or two group members to each Christian denomination and each other religion you wish to explore. Have them lead a meeting or part of a meeting. We provide a list of good resources at the end of this section to help with research. We also strongly recommend that you seek out experts in the field to attend your men's group for these particular discussions. Invite a minister or community leader from a local Lutheran, Methodist, or Adventist church. Seek out leaders from a local temple or mosque. Maybe approach someone from a nearby college or university to attend. The discussion questions and exercises below are designed to spark discussion, but the group will be best served by listening to people who are steeped in their faith.

Opening Prayer

Lord, you speak to us in Leviticus 19—"love your neighbor as yourself."
Help us enter our time together today with open minds and hearts
and the genuine desire to understand the beliefs of all your children. Please bring us the compassion, humility, and inquisitiveness
that will help us be examples to others
of how to accept our fellow human beings.
We pray this in your name.
Amen.

Humor

A priest, a rabbi, a minister, and a monk walked into a bar and the bartender asked, "What is this, a joke?"

Guidance

As the world becomes increasingly interconnected, a broad range of cultures collide and mingle on a daily basis. Yet if we watch the news, we see a lot more colliding than mingling. If anything, the news emphasizes our differences and very often portrays religion primarily as a vehicle for conflict, even violence. Beliefs are pitted against each other in culture wars all over the globe and the results can bring feelings of hopelessness. Lost in the conflict is the message of harmony and peace that lies at the heart of the world's great religions. What is lost is God. Instead, we must take the time to seek God in others through their faiths. As we do, we will discover some fundamental elements we have in common. For example, a central tenet of Judaism, Christianity, and Islam is the belief in one God or monotheism. Moreover adherents of these great faiths share a common claim as the children of Abraham. All the world's major religions preach both compassion for the poor and a duty to abide by God's law. By understanding these similarities, as well as the differences, we will better appreciate our own path to God in Catholic Christianity and, hopefully, discover our common bonds with others who seek God. As stewards of God's grace on earth, we have an obligation to understand the beliefs of all his children, not just the ones within our own faith community.

Passage From Scripture

> If anyone thinks he is religious and does not bridle his tongue but deceives his heart, his religion is vain. Religion that is pure and undefiled before God and the Father is this: to care for orphans and widows in their affliction and to keep oneself unstained by the world.
>
> —James 1:26–27

Food for Thought

> God made Truth with many doors to welcome every believer who knocks on them.
>
> —Kahlil Gibran

Discussion and Journaling *(as group or in pairs)*

For each religion you address, try to answer the following questions.

1. What, if anything, about this religion (or other Christian church) do you find appealing? What might we learn from it?

2. What aspects of Christianity (or Catholicism) do you appreciate even more now that you know, at least a little, about the religion (or other Christian church) in question?

Exercise *(discuss as group or in pairs)*

For each religion or other church you choose to discuss, try the following exercise. Identify those elements that are similar to Christianity or Catholicism as well as those that are different. While acknowledging the differences, discuss what you feel might be common ground. Identify ways you might reach out to people of these faiths or churches and build bridges.

Journal Notes

Additional Reading

Abraham: A Journey to the Heart of the Three Faiths by Bruce Feiler

The Complete Idiot's Guide to World Religions by Brandon Toropov and Father Luke Buckles

Great Religions of the World by Merle Severy

The World's Religions by Huston Smith

World Religions: Western Traditions by Willard G. Oxtoby

3.

SPIRITUAL COMMUNITY LEADERSHIP

Objective: *To discuss the impact of sharing our faith with those around us and to share group insights on the concept of evangelization, examining the pros and cons of wearing one's faith on one's sleeve.*

Preparation

Come to this meeting with stories of how you or others have found Christ. Be prepared to share your thoughts about the range of ways you share your faith with others.

Opening Prayer

Lord, each day we have the chance to live our
lives as Jesus asks
and to share our belief in the Good News when
opportunities arise.
Teach us to look for these moments
when we can share our love for you with others.
Help us overcome shyness, embarrassment, and
worry
as excuses to remain silent when our words can
be so valuable to others.
Fill us with the Holy Spirit
so that we can live our lives as examples of your
Word.
Amen.

Humor

> A priest is evangelizing at the local pub. He goes up to the first man sitting at the bar and says, "Son, would you like to go to heaven?"
>
> "Yes, Father."
>
> "Then go stand over against the wall."
>
> The priest goes to the second man, "Son, would you like to go to heaven?"
>
> "Yes, Father."
>
> "Then go and stand over against the wall."
>
> The priest goes up to the third man, "Son, would you like to go to heaven?"
>
> "Ah, no thanks!" says the man.
>
> The priest is astounded. "You don't want to go to heaven when you die?"
>
> "Oh, when I die, sure!" says the man. "I thought you were getting a group together to go now."

Guidance

The original spiritual leaders of Christianity were so committed to sharing their personal experience with Christ that they were willing to risk their lives for the opportunity. In many places of the world, that depth of commitment continues today. As members of the Church we have a great opportunity and a great mission to spread the Good News—rarely with even the slightest risk to our lives. The question is: how do we go about doing this?

There is no single right answer of course because everyone has unique traits and needs that will affect how different people promote or receive the Word of God. However, a saying commonly attributed to St. Francis of Assisi offers a useful approach: "Preach the gospel at all times. Use words if necessary." What this means is that the most effective way we can share the Word is to visibly and openly live the Word. We are called to share the light of Christ and to have faith that people will take notice. Yet, with so many other things commanding people's attention, it can be hard to ensure that people see and feel the presence of God in their hearts. Here, we take the time to share our personal experiences with each side of evangelization, from conversion to converting, and discuss what seems to work best in our communities.

Passage From Scripture

For if anyone is a hearer of the Word and not a doer, he is like a man who looks at his own face in a mirror. He sees himself, then goes off and promptly forgets what he looked like. But the one who peers into the perfect law of freedom and perseveres, and is not a hearer who forgets but a doer who acts, such a one shall be blessed in what he does.

—James 1:23–25

Food for Thought

You must be the change you wish to see in the world.

—Mahatma Gandhi

Discussion and Journaling *(as group or in pairs)*

1. Research suggests that the largest religious group in almost every U.S. community is non-practicing Christians. Why do you think this is so? Discuss ways in which your parish could do a better job of reaching out to these people.

2. On a more personal level, do you live your life in such a way as to set an example for others? Do you think you live your life as Jesus would want you to?

How do you feel about sharing your faith with others? What are some situations in which you were glad you shared your faith and felt you made a difference in someone's life?

3. How do other church communities approach evangelization? What can we learn from them? Discuss different techniques for evangelization—from knocking on doors to simply serving as a role model in the community. What ways do you think are most effective? Is there room for improvement?

Exercise *(discuss as group or in pairs)*

Share stories of how you or others found a home in your parish. Was the process slow or sudden? Was the conversion linked to a particular relationship or did you take the leap on your own? Discuss what we might learn from this process. What can we do to make our personal or our parish's approach to evangelization more meaningful and productive. If you have an evangelization committee at your parish, consider sharing your thoughts with them. If church attendance is stagnating or declining, parish leaders may be receptive to new ideas and a new approach. Consider getting involved.

Journal Notes

Additional Reading

The Art of Personal Evangelism by Will McRaney
Courageous Leadership by Bill Hybels
Just Walk Across the Room by Bill Hybels
United States Conference of Catholic Bishops at
www.usccb.org/evangelization

WEALTH AND
CHARITY

For one or two meetings

Objective: *To recognize that we are stewards of our own fortune, however large or small that may be.*

Preparation

Make a mental calculation of your tangible and intangible assets.

Opening Prayer

Lord, you have taught us that where our treasure is,
there our hearts will be also.
As we spend time today discussing the contrast between wealth and charity,
help us consider our definitions of wealth
and our motivations for accumulating passions.
Help us understand where our true "treasure" in life resides.
We pray this in the name of the Father, the Son, and the Holy Spirit.
Amen.

Humor

Mrs. Applebee posed this problem to one of her fifth-grade classes: "A wealthy man dies and leaves behind ten million dollars. One-fifth is to go to his wife, one-fifth to his son, one-sixth to his butler, and the rest to charity. Now, what does each get?" After a long silence in the classroom, Johnny raised his hand and answered "A lawyer!"

Guidance

We all know what Jesus thinks about money—or at least we think we do. In the first three gospels he says, "It is easier for a camel to pass through (the) eye of (a) needle than for one who is rich to enter the kingdom of God" (Mt 19:24, Mk 10:25, Lk 18:25). Yet it is not money, per se, that prevents people from union with God. It is our misuse and even obsession with it. "For the love of money is the root of all evils, and some people in their desire for it have strayed from the faith and have pierced themselves with many pains" (1 Tm 6:10). And as Ecclesiastes states quite clearly, "The covetous man is never satisfied with money, and the lover of wealth reaps no fruit from it; so this too is vanity" (Eccl 5:9). The power of money draws us away from God, and our own weakness allows wealth to become an idol for worship.

In Matthew's story of the rich young man (Mt 19: 16–30), Jesus indicates the power money has over even the best of intentions. In this story Jesus meets a young man who obeys the Ten Commandments but wants to do more to ensure his place in heaven. When Christ tells him to sell his possessions and give to the poor, the man cannot do it. Money has too strong a hold over him. Which brings us to the dual power of charity. Charity—the giving of our time and treasure out of love for others—is a single action that helps both the less fortunate and ourselves, by helping to release us from the power of money.

Money itself is not evil. Both Jesus and Paul were the beneficiaries of wealthy believers. But one can be sure that these ancient donors benefited at least as much as the recipients did. We are asked only to give what we can—Jesus recognized the widow who gave only two copper coins as a great benefactor (Mk 12:41–44)—but we are asked to give just the same. When we give sincerely, out of our hearts, we will receive our true reward (Mt 6: 1–4).

Points to consider:

- It is up to those of us who "have" to consider those of use who "have not."
- Sometimes defining if you are a "have" or a "have-not" is hard.
- Wealth can make us somewhat blind—the more we have, the more we want.
- Living a simple life with less power and wealth can be freeing.
- Money itself is not evil, but how our hearts are shaped around it can be.
- Charity begins with a focus on others' needs and letting go of our need for possessions.
- In the end God is lending us everything in our lives anyhow! We can't take it with us when we leave. We might as well share it while we're here.

Passage From Scripture

No one can serve two masters. He will either hate one and love the other, or be devoted to one and despise the other. You cannot serve God and [money].

—Matthew 6:24

Food for Thought

> If a free society cannot help the many who are
> poor, it cannot save the few who are rich.
>   —John F. Kennedy

Discussion and Journaling *(as group or in pairs)*

1. Does money have power over you? What are some possessions in your life that you honestly believe it would be hard to go without? Why?

2. When is "enough, enough?" Can you think of examples of people who never seem to have enough? What about examples for your own family? Do feelings of greed, jealousy, or even despair fester in you because you worry that you will never have enough? What steps can you take to avoid these and reconnect with the true power of faith?

3. To what groups or social causes do you give your time and treasure? To which do you want to give? What are the criteria you and your family use for giving? Take time to discuss the charities to which you give.

4. If you're inspired, consider taking up a collection for a particular charity that may be made on behalf of your faith group. Discuss local, national, or international options appropriate for group giving. Have fun exploring and making your selection.

Exercise

In pairs or in your journal, make a list of your intangible assets. These may include family love, free time, time for your children, pride in yourself, friends, your ability to give to charity, etc. Next, make a list of your tangible assets: income, house, car, etc. Now, take a moment to consider to what degree your tangible assets may actually serve as liabilities against your intangible assets. In other words, do your car and mortgage payments detract from your ability to spend time on your intangible treasures? When complete, discuss with the other members of the group.

Journal Notes

Additional Reading

Banker to the Poor by Muhammad Yunus

A Concise Guide to Catholic Social Teaching by Kevin E. McKenna

Deus Caritas Est (God is Love) by Pope Benedict XVI

Giving by John Ortberg, Laurie Pederson, and Judson Poling

The Power of Generosity by Dave Toycen

You Did It for Me: Care of Your Neighbor as a Spiritual Practice by Kevin E. McKenna

Wealth Conundrum by Ralph Doudera

5.

GROUP COMMUNITY SERVICE

For one or two meetings

Objective: *To consider opportunities of significance for your entire group that are right in front of you, at work and in the community.*

Preparation

Identify an organization or cause to which your group can give its time and talent. Refer to the organizations identified in the first meeting of this chapter for inspiration. Bring your suggestions to the meeting and prepare to discuss how you can get involved as a group.

Opening Prayer

Gracious Lord,
as a faith group we have learned the power
of a diverse set of opinions, thoughts, and prayers.
We've enjoyed our friendships as they've deepened
with the guidance of the Holy Spirit.
Now we seek to think about things outside our group,
outside of ourselves.
Help us open up our eyes to opportunities to make an impact
on our local community or in the larger world.

Guide us to good deeds in your name.
Amen.

Humor

Sure I'm for helping the elderly. I'm going to be
old myself some day.

—Lillian Carter, while in her eighties

Guidance

A man beseeches God that there are too many problems in the world and wonders why the good Lord
seems unable or unwilling to fix them. To the man's complete surprise, God answers: "That's why I sent you."
This is an old story that reminds us of our role as God's
stewards on earth. We have a limited amount of time in
our lives and there are, God knows, too many problems
to address. Fortunately, the group of men sitting with
you now are more than capable of doing, solving, fixing, or generally sprucing up just about anything. Our
own men's faith group, the Boys of Breakfast, has found
a number of ways to give back to the community. These
have ranged from fixing up an old Boy Scouts camp to
raising funds for local charities. We enjoyed the camaraderie and benefited at least as much as those we tried
to help. Now, having walked together in faith to center
ourselves with God, nurture a better faith life with our
family, and seek out faith in our workplace, it's time
to look around the room and ask what can be done for
the community. The world will truly be a better place
because of your efforts.

Passage From Scripture

Then the righteous will answer him and say,
"Lord, when did we see you hungry and feed
you, or thirsty and give you drink? When did we

see you a stranger and welcome you, or naked and clothe you? When did we see you ill or in prison, and visit you?" And the king will say to them in reply, "Amen, I say to you, whatever you did for one of these least brothers of mine, you did for me."

—Matthew 25:37–40

Food for Thought

Never doubt that a small group of thought-ful, committed citizens can change the world. Indeed, it is the only thing that ever has.

—Margaret Mead

Discussion and Journaling *(as group or in pairs)*

1. Think of community service projects you have admired. What are the qualities of these projects you most admire? Examples might be Scouting projects, church programs, local government activities, neighborhood efforts, non-profit projects, fundraising efforts, etc. What lessons can you apply to a proposed community project?

2. Why is it an essential call of our baptism to offer ourselves in service? Do you feel good when you are involved in giving back to the community (be honest)? Why or why not? What can be done so that you may give in order to truly receive?

Exercise

This exercise is simple, but will take time to implement. Discuss the community service suggestions brought by members of the group. Next have the group brainstorm other ideas for local service opportunities. Have someone write these down. Next, ask group members how much time they are willing to commit and what day within the next month or so they are available. Try to reach consensus about which of the ideas you will pursue as a group. Commit to doing it and agree on a point person to contact the selected organization and volunteer your group to help. Don't forget to report back to the group at subsequent meetings on this last task. And have fun.

Journal Notes

Additional Reading

Becoming a Community of Salt and Light by Peggy Prevoznik Heins

Communities of Salt and Light: Reflections on the Social Mission of the Parish by the United States Conference of Catholic Bishops

Parish Social Ministry by Tom Ulrich

The Random Acts of Kindness Foundation, www.actsofkindness.org

Acknowledgments

We'd like to express our unending gratitude to our families. Steve is grateful to Meri for her undying love and editorial support, to his children for keeping him young, and to his entire extended family for constantly reinforcing the importance of relationships. Randy appreciates the foundation that Patty brings to his life. He has learned most of his best life-balancing habits from her and from his children, Kayla, Julianna, and Elise.

We thank the original Boys of Breakfast: Scott Clayton, Mark Keckeis, Frank Marotto, Jack Porter, Russ Schafer, Kevin Harrington, Mike Kimball, John Kurtzweil, and Tom Wessel. Without you, nothing would have bloomed! Thanks for planting the seeds.

We'd like to thank the additional Boys of Breakfast who have been with us in our first seven years: Bob Athenour, Greg Avalos, Mark Buck, Ed Burkart, Pete Defao, John Duddy, Dave Freitas, Tom Fristoe, Bing Hadley, Mike Gallagher, Don Landsittel, Jim Pease, Dom Pietro, Ed Pitts, Mike Regan, Rob Royea, Michael Schwab, Carl Schlachte, Frank Spindler, Dave Stiehr, Fred Trevor, Frank Vaculin, and Pete Yozzo. Thank you for gathering every other Tuesday to share breakfast, faith, and a few laughs, and for your spiritual guidance and shared fellowship.

Most particularly, we would like to thank Ed Burkart for leading the jokes at every meeting and Mike Gallagher for frequently leading prayer—your contributions are included throughout. Our parish, the Catholic Community of Pleasanton, has provided an excellent foundation for our journey in faith. A particular word of thanks goes to Fr. Dan Danielson and Fr. Padraig Green for their insights and guidance and to our other spiritual mentors: Fr. Mark Wiesner, Fr. Tony Herrera, Fr. Paul Minnihan, Karen Miller, John Mabry, Gregory Slayton, and Pat Sullivan. We thank you for joining our group on occasion and sharing your knowledge.

Special gratitude goes to the staff at Jim's, Vic's, Zorn's, and Baker's Square for providing needed coffee, oatmeal, and a morning smile over the years.

We thank everyone who helped to get the words right. We benefited from a number of readers, including Alex Brubaker, Ed Burkart, Bing Hadley, Patty Haykin, John McCrea, Meri McCoy-Thompson, Lloyd Reeb, Dave Stiehr, Russ Schafer, and Gregory Slayton. Thanks also to Eileen Ponder, our editor at Ave Maria Press, and to Bob Hamma, for believing in our message to men.

Above all, we praise God for the abundance, balance, and guidance that he has given us in our lives.

Steve McCoy-Thompson is co-founder of the Boys of Breakfast men's faith group in Pleasanton, California, and president of Community to People, a non-profit micro bridge lending organization. He has authored numerous articles on business concerns and change leadership as well as two books, *Weather Boy: A Story of D-Day* and *Journey into Belief*, which details the story of his conversion to Christianity. McCoy-Thompson holds degrees from Duke University and the Fletcher School at Tufts University. A successful businessman and parish leader, he lives with his wife Meri and their children, Matthias and Marie, in the San Francisco Bay area.

Randy M. Haykin is an accomplished Silicon Valley entrepreneur and venture capitalist, who has been involved in numerous start-ups such as Yahoo, Overture, eCircles, and My eLife. He has also been a spiritual leader in his community in the Bay Area, forming the first men's group Boys of Breakfast in 2001, after converting from Judaism to Catholicism. Haykin graduated from Brown University with a degree in Organizational Behavior and Management, and also holds an MBA from Harvard Business School. Haykin is on the Leadership Council for the American Cancer Society and is on the Board of Governors for Opportunity International, an organization that works with impoverished entrepreneurs in twenty-nine countries around the world through micro-lending and social entrepreneurshp. Haykin's primary focus in life is his marriage to Patty of twenty-plus years, and being a great dad for his three daughters: Elise, Julianna, and Kayla.